Masonic Ritual and Monitor

PART TWO

TO THE DEGREES OF MARK MASTER, PAST MASTER,
MOST EXCELLENT MASTER, AND THE ROYAL ARCH

BY

MALCOLM C. DUNCAN

EXPLAINED AND INTERPRETED BY COPIOUS
NOTES AND NUMEROUS ENGRAVINGS

REVISED EDITION

Printed in Canada

MARK MASTER, OR FOURTH DEGREE

THE Degree of Mark Master,, which is the Fourth in the Masonic series, is, historically considered, of the utmost importance, since we are informed that, by its influence, each operative Mason, at the building of King Solomon's Temple, was known and distinguished, and the disorder and confusion which might otherwise have attended so immense an undertaking was completely prevented, and not only the craftsmen themselves, but every part of their workmanship was discriminated with the greatest nicety and the utmost facility.

It is claimed by Masonic writers,[1] that this Degree in Masonry was instituted by King Solomon, at the building of the Temple, for the purpose of detecting impostors, while paying wages to the craftsmen. Each operative was required to put his mark upon the product of his labor, and these distinctive marks were all known to the Senior Grand Warden. If any of the workmanship was found to be defective, it was a matter of no difficulty for the overseers to ascertain at once who was the imperfect craftsman, and remedy the defect. Thus the faulty workman was punished, without diminishing the wages of the diligent and faithful craftsmen. A candidate upon whom this Degree has been conferred is said to have been "advanced to the honorary Degree of Mark Master."

Eight officers are necessary to open a Lodge in this Degree, viz.:

1. R. W. Master; 2. S. G. Warden; 3. J. G. Warden; 4. Senior Deacon; 5. Junior Deacon; 6. Master Overseer; 7. Senior Overseer; 8. Junior Overseer.

---

[1] This Degree is said to have been instituted to detect impostors, in paying the wages to the craftsmen, as we have just seen. It is a well-known fact, that such a system of distinction was practised in the Masonry of all ages. Mr. Godwin, speaking of buildings of more modern construction than the Temple of Solomon, says: "The marks, it can hardly be doubted, were made to distinguish the work of different individuals. At the present time, the man who works a stone (being different from the man who sets it) makes his mark on the bed or other internal face of it, so that it may be identified.—*Historical Landmarks*, vol. I., p. 427.

The officers of a Chapter rank as follows, viz.: the High Priest, as R. W. Master; King, as Senior Grand Warden; Scribe, as Junior Grand Warden; Captain of the Host, as Master of Ceremonies; Principal Sojourner, as Senior Deacon; Royal Arch Captain, as Junior Deacon; Master of the Third Veil, as Master Overseer; Master of the Second Veil, as Senior Overseer; Master of the First Veil, as Junior Overseer. The Treasurer, Secretary, and Tyler, corresponding in rank with the same officers in other Degrees. These officers are filled by the officers of the Chapter under whose warrant the Lodge is held.

The symbolic color of the Mark Degree is purple. The apron is of white lambskin, edged with purple, and the collar of purple, edged with gold. But as Mark Lodges are no longer independent bodies, but always held under the warrant of a Royal Arch Chapter, the collars, aprons, and jewels of the Chapter are generally made use of in conferring the Mark Degree.

Lodges of Mark Masters are "dedicated to Hiram, the Builder."

The interior arrangements of the Lodge, and the positions of the Master, Wardens, Deacons, Secretary, and Treasurer, are the same as those in the Entered Apprentices' Degree (p. 8). The Master Overseer takes his seat on the right of the Right Worshipful Master in the east. The Senior Overseer sits on the right of the Senior Grand Warden in the west, and his Junior on the right of the Junior Grand Warden in the south.

Right Worshipful Master (giving a rap with his gavel).— Brethren, I am about to open a Lodge of Mark Master Masons in this place, for the dispatch of business. I will thank you for your attention and assistance. If there is any person present who has not taken this Degree, he is requested to retire.

To Senior Grand Warden:

Brother Senior, are you satisfied that all present are Mark Masters?

S. G. W.—Right Worshipful, I wish the pass-word might be given by the brethren.

The two Deacons thereupon go round and receive the word, which is JOPPA, in the same manner as in the Master Mason's Degree (p. 20).

R. W. M. (giving one rap).—Brother Junior Deacon, the first care of congregated Masons?

J. D. (rising on his feet, and, at the same time, giving a sign— see Fig. 20, p. 153). — To see the Lodge tyled, Right Worshipful.

R. W. M.—Perform that part of your duty, and inform the Tyler that we are about to open a Lodge of Mark Master Masons in this place, for the dispatch of business; and direct him to tyle accordingly.

The Junior Deacon then walks rapidly to the door, and gives four raps (● ● ● ●), which are answered by four without from the Tyler; the Junior Deacon gives one, which is answered by the Tyler with (●); the door is then partly opened, when the Junior Deacon delivers his message. He then returns, gives the sign (see Fig. 20, p. 153) again, and says:

The door is tyled, Right Worshipful.

R. W. M.—How tyled?

J. D.—Within the outer door, by a brother of this Degree, with a drawn sword in his hand.

R. W. M.—His duty there?

J. D.—To keep off all cowans and eavesdroppers, see that none pass or repass without due qualification, or permission from the Right Worshipful Master.

R. W. M.—Let us be clothed, brethren.

Here the officers and members put on their aprons and jewels. The Master gives two raps with his gavel, which brings all the subordinate officers on their feet; and each, standing in his place, recites his duty on being questioned.

R. W. M.—The Junior Overseer's station in the Lodge?

J. O.—At the south gate.

R. W. M.—Your duty there, Brother Junior Overseer?

J. O.—To inspect all materials brought up for the building of the Temple; and, if approved, pass them on to the Senior Overseer, at the west gate, for further inspection.

R. W. M.—The Senior Overseer's place in the Lodge?

S. O.—At the west gate.

R. W. M.—Your business there, Brother Senior Overseer?

S. O.—To inspect all materials brought up for the building of the Temple, and, if approved, pass them on to the Master Overseer, at the east gate, for further inspection.

R. W. M.—The Master Overseer's place in the Lodge?

M. O.—At the east gate.

R. W. M.—Your business there, Brother Master Overseer?

M. O.—To preside at the inspection of all materials brought up for the building of the Temple; and, if disapproved, to call a council of my brother Overseers.

R. W. M.—The Junior Deacon's place in the Lodge?

J. D.—At the right, in front of the Senior Grand Warden.

R. W. M.—Your duty there, Brother Junior?

J. D.—To carry messages from the Senior Grand Warden in the west to the Junior Grand Warden in the south, and elsewhere about the Lodge as he may direct.

R. W. M.—The Senior Deacon's place in the Lodge?

S. D.—At the right, in front of the Right Worshipful Master in the east.

R. W. M.—Your duty there, Brother Senior?

S. D.—To carry messages from the Right Worshipful Master in the east to the Senior Grand Warden in the west, and elsewhere about the Lodge, as he may direct; to assist in the preparation and initiation of candidates; and to welcome and clothe all visiting brethren.

R. W. M.—The Secretary's station in the Lodge?

Sec.—At the left hand of the Right Worshipful Master in the east.

R. W. M.—Your duty there, Brother Secretary?

Sec.—To record the doings of the Lodge, collect all money, pay it over to the Treasurer, and keep a true and correct account of the same.

R. W. M.—The Treasurer's station in the Lodge?

Treas.—At the right hand of the Worshipful Master in the east.

R. W. M.—Your duty there, Brother Treasurer?

Treas.—To receive all money from the hands of the Secretary, to keep a true and correct account of the same, and pay it out by order of the Right Worshipful Master, with the consent of the brethren.

R. W. M.—The Junior Grand Warden's place in the Lodge?

J. G. W.—In the south, Right Worshipful.

R. W. M.—Your duty there, Brother Junior?

J. G. W.—As the sun is in the south at high twelve, which is the glory and beauty of the day, so stands the Junior Grand Warden in the south, to call the crafts from labor to refreshment, and from refreshment to labor, that the Right Worshipful Master may have profit and pleasure thereby.

R. W. M.—The Senior Grand Warden's place in the Lodge?

S. G. W.—In the west, Right Worshipful.

R. W. M.—Your duty there, Brother Senior?

S. G. W.—As the sun sets in the west, to close the day, so stands the Senior Grand Warden in the west, to assist the Right Worshipful Master in opening and closing his Lodge, pay the crafts their wages, if any be due, and see that none go away dissatisfied; harmony being the strength and support of all institutions, but more especially of ours.

R. W. M. — The Right Worshipful Master's Station in the Lodge?

S. G. W.—In the east, Right Worshipful.

R. W. M.—His duty there, Brother Senior?

S. G. W.—As the sun rises in the east, to open and adorn the day, so rises the Right Worshipful Master in the east to open and adorn his Lodge, and set the craft to work, with proper instructions for their labor.

R. W. M. (rising).—After that manner so do I. It is my will and pleasure that a Lodge of Mark Master Masons be opened in. this place, for the dispatch of business. Brother Senior, you will please communicate the same to the Junior Grand Warden

FIG. 19   FIG. 20

THE "HEAVE-OVER"   SIGN OF A MARK MASTER

in the south, that the brethren may have due and timely notice thereof.

S. G. W. (to Junior).—Brother Junior, it is the Right Worshipful Master's order that a Lodge of Mark Master Masons be opened in this place, for the dispatch of business. You will please inform the brethren thereof.

J. G. W. (giving three raps with the gavel (● ● ●).—Brethren, it is the Right Worshipful Master's order that a Lodge of Mark Master Masons be opened in this place, for the dispatch of business. You are ordered to take due notice thereof, and govern yourselves accordingly.

R. W. M.—Attend to the signs, brethren.

Here the Right Worshipful Master gives all the signs, in their regular order, from the Entered Apprentice to Mark Master, the brethren all imitating him. (For signs of the Entered Apprentice, or First Degree, see Figs. 1 and 2; for signs of the Fellow Craft, or Second Degree, see Figs. 3 and 4; and for signs of Master Mason, or Third Degree, see Figs. 5, 6, and 7, pp. 16, 17, and 18.)

After the duegard and sign of the Entered Apprentice, the duegard and sign of the Fellow Craft, and the duegard, sign, and grand hailing sign of the Master Mason are given in their regular order, then the Mark Master's signs are given. First, the HEAVE-OVER, which is given as follows:

Place the flat back of the *right* hand in the flat palm of the *left* hand, and hold them down in front opposite to the *right* hip, then bring them up to the left shoulder with a quick motion, as though you were throwing something over your left shoulder. In putting your hands together, do so with a sharp slap, the *palms* facing your shoulder. In old times this sign was made by interlacing the fingers. (See Richardson's *Monitor*.) This sign is called the Heave-over, and alludes to the rejection of the keystone in this Degree. (See Fig. 19.)

The second sign is made as follows:

After having made the first sign, drop the arms to each side of the body, and clinch the last two fingers of the right hand, leaving the first two and thumb open, parallel with each other, and about one inch apart. This alludes to the manner in which the candidate is directed to carry the keystone. You then raise the right hand rapidly to the right ear, still holding the thumb and first two fingers open, and with a circular motion of the hand pass the fingers around the ear, as though you were combing back your earlock, the ear passing between the two fingers and thumb. (See Fig. 20.) This sign alludes to a penalty of the obligation, to have the ear smitten off.

After having completed the sign, as just described, drop the right hand a little to the right side, about as high up as the waist, the palm open and horizontal, and, at the same time, lift up the left hand and bring it down edgewise and vertically upon the wrist of the right. (See Fig. 21.) These motions must all be made distinctly but rapidly. This sign alludes to the penalty of the obligation, and also to that of an impostor, which is to have his right hand cut off.

The sign of receiving wages is made by extending in front the right arm at full length, the thumb and two first fingers open, about one inch apart, the third and little fingers clinched, palm of the hand up. (See Fig. 22.) It alludes to the peculiar manner in which the Mark Master is taught to receive wages, so that impostors may be detected.

Here it is proper to remark that in the opening of any Lodge of Masons, they commence giving the signs of an Entered Apprentice, and go through all the signs of the different Degrees,

FIG. 21   FIG. 22

SECOND SIGN OF A MARK MASTER   SIGN OF RECEIVING WAGES

in regular gradation, until they arrive at the one which they are opening, and commence at the sign of the Degree in which they are at work, and descend to the last when closing.

The Master now reads from a text-book the following:

"Wherefore, my brethren, lay aside all malice, and guile, and hypocrisies, and envies, and all evil speaking. If so be ye have tasted that the Lord is gracious; to whom coming, as unto a living stone, disallowed indeed of men, but chosen of God, and precious; ye also, as living stones, be ye built up a spiritual house, an holy priesthood, to offer up sacrifices acceptable to God. Brethren, this is the will of God, that with well-doing ye put to silence the ignorance of foolish men. As free, and not as using your liberty for a cloak of maliciousness, but as the servants of God. Honor all men, love the brotherhood, fear God."

The Right Worshipful Master then gives two raps with his gavel, Senior Grand Warden two, and Junior Grand Warden two, which raps are then repeated.

R. W. M.—I now declare this Lodge of Mark Master Masons opened in due and ancient form, and hereby forbid all improper conduct whereby this Lodge may be disturbed, under no less penalty than the by-laws of a majority of the Lodge may see fit to inflict.

R. W. M. (to Junior Deacon).—Brother Junior, please to inform the Tyler the Lodge is open.

Junior Deacon informs the Tyler, and returns to his seat.

No business is done in a Lodge of Mark Master Masons, except to initiate a candidate in the Fourth Degree of Masonry. The Degree being under the sanction of the Royal Arch Chapter, all business, such as balloting for candidates committee reports, &c., is done in the Seventh, or Royal Arch Degree. The Lodge being opened, and ready for such business as it has authority to transact, the Right Worshipful Master directs the Senior Deacon to ascertain if there are any candidates desiring to be advanced to the honorary Degree of Mark Master Mason. The Senior Deacon then retires to the ante-room, and if he finds any candidates in waiting, he returns to the Lodge and informs the Right Worshipful Master. It is the duty of the Senior Deacon to prepare and conduct the candidate (or candidates, as the case may be), during the first part of the ceremony of initiation, and if there are any candidates for advancement, the Right Worshipful Master directs this officer to retire to the ante-room and see them duly and truly prepared. The Junior Deacon, with an assistant, then passes out of the Lodge into the ante-room, where the candidate is in waiting (we will suppose that only one is to be advanced), and requests him to divest himself of his coat and roll up his shirt-sleeves to the shoulder. The Senior Deacon and his associate do the same. When they are thus prepared, the Deacon takes in his right hand a small block of marble or painted wood, about the size of a brick, weighing five or six pounds. The Deacon's associate also takes a similar block to carry. One of the blocks has a square engraved upon it, the other, a plumb. (See cut.) The candidate is then furnished with a block representing a keystone, which he is requested to carry between the thumb and two first fingers of the right hand, the other fingers clinched with the nails tight against the palm, the arm extended down perpendicularly at the side. The two officers carry their blocks in the same manner. The three are styled "Workmen from the quarries." As we have before said, the block which the candidate carries represents a keystone, and has the initials H. T. W. S. S. T. K. S. engraved upon it in a circle.

Sometimes this stone weighs twelve or fifteen pounds, and it is considered a very nice job to carry a block of this weight *plumb.* The blocks which the conductors carry are usually made of wood, and are, therefore, comparatively light. The three "workmen" now form in a line about three feet distant from each other, the candidate being last. The door is then opened without ceremony, and the Junior Deacon, as conductor, together with his associate and the candidate, enter the Lodge, and march four times around the room, halting the last time at the Junior Overseer's station, at the south gate, where the conductor gives four raps (in couplets) on the floor with his heel (● ● ● ●).

1.   2.   3.

WORKMEN FROM THE QUARRIES

Junior Overseer—Who comes here?

Senior Deacon—Workmen from the quarries, bringing up work.

Junior Overseer—Have you a specimen of your work?

Senior Deacon—We have.

Junior Overseer—Present your work.

The Senior Deacon presents his stone to the Junior Overseer, who applies his small trying square to its different angles, and, they agreeing with the angles of the square, he says:

Junior Overseer—This is good work—square work—just such work as we are authorized to receive for the building (returning the block to the Senior Deacon). You will pass on to the Senior Overseer at the west gate, for further inspection.

The second workman then presents his block, and it is tried and returned the same as the conductor's.

The two workmen move on about six paces, in order to bring the candidate before the Junior Overseer's station. The Junior Deacon then instructs the candidate how to make the alarm and present his work.

Junior Overseer—Who comes here?

Candidate (prompted).—A craftsman from the quarries, bringing you work.

Junior Overseer—Have you a specimen of your work?

Candidate—I have.

Junior Overseer—Present it.

Candidate presents the keystone.

Junior Overseer (applying his square to it, and finding it does not fit).—This is a curiously wrought stone, indeed; it is neither oblong nor square; good work, true work, square work is only such as we have orders to receive; neither has it the mark of any of the craft upon it. Is that your mark? (Pointing to the letters on the keystone.)

Candidate—It is not.

Junior Overseer—Owing to its singular form and beauty, I feel unwilling to reject it; you will pass on to the Senior Overseer at the west gate for his inspection.

The conductors and the candidate pass on to the Senior Overseer's station in the west, when the same scene is repeated, and they are directed to proceed to the Master Overseer at the east gate.

The Senior Deacon here first presents his block or stone to the Master Overseer.

Master Overseer (applying his square).—This is good work, true work, and square work—just such work as I am authorized to receive and pass for the building. You are entitled to your wages—pass on.

The conductors pass on, and take their seats. The candidate then presents his keystone.

Master Overseer (applying his square).—This is a curiously wrought stone. It appears to be neither oblong nor square, and the mark upon it is not that of a craftsman. (Looking sternly at candidate.) Is this your work?

Candidate—It is not.

Master Overseer—Where did you get it?

Candidate—I picked it up in the quarry.

Master Overseer—Why do you bring another man's work to impose upon the Overseers? You will stand aside.

The Master Overseer now stamps on the floor four times with his foot, which brings up the other two Overseers.

Master Overseer—Brother Junior Overseer, did you suffer this work to pass your inspection?

Junior Overseer—I did; I observed to the young craftsman, at the time, that the stone was not such as we had orders to receive; but, owing to its singular form and beauty, I felt unwilling to reject it, and suffered it to pass to the Senior Overseer at the west gate.

Senior Overseer—I made the same observations to the young craftsman, and for the same reason permitted it to pass to the Master Overseer at the east gate.

R. W. M.—Why, you see the stone is neither oblong nor square, neither has it the mark of any of the craft upon it. Do you know this mark that is upon it?

Junior Overseer—I do not.

Senior Overseer—Neither do I.

Master Overseer—What shall I do with it?

Junior Overseer—I propose we heave it over among the rubbish.[1]

Master Overseer—Agreed.

The Master and Senior Overseers take up the keystone, and swinging it four times back and forth between them, the fourth time the Junior Overseer catches it over the left shoulder of the Master Overseer (in imitation of the sign of "heave-over," see Fig. 19), and throws it aside. At this moment all the brethren begin to shuffle around the room, leaving their seats.

R. W. M. (giving one rap with his gavel).—What is the cause of this disturbance among the workmen?

S. G. W.—It is the sixth hour of the sixth day of the week, and the craft are impatient to receive their wages.

The whole Lodge here rise to their feet and sing the following:

"Another six days' work is done,
  Another Sabbath has begun;
  Return, my soul, enjoy thy rest,
  Improve the hours thy God hath blest."

R. W. M.—Brother Senior Grand Warden, it is my order that

---

[1] By the influence of the Mark Master's Degree, the work of every operative Mason was distinctly known. The perfect stones were received with acclamations; while those that were deficient, were rejected with disdain. This arrangement proved a superior stimulus to exertion, which accounts for the high finish which the Temple subsequently acquired.—*Historical Landmarks*, vol. i. p. 421.

you assemble the craft, and march in procession to the office of the Senior Grand Warden, to receive wages.

The members now form two and two (candidate behind), and march round the Lodge, singing the song:

MARK MASTER'S SONG
TUNE— "America"

Mark Masters, all appear
Before the Chief O'erseer:
   In concert move;
Let him your work inspect,
For the Chief Architect,
If there be no defect,
   He will approve.

You who have passed the square,
For your rewards prepare,
   Join heart and hand;
Each with his mark in view,
March with the just and true,
Wages to you are due,
   At your command.

Hiram, the widow's son,
Sent unto Solomon
   Our great keystone:
On it appears the name
Which raises high the fame
Of all to whom the same
   Is truly known.

Now to the westward move,
Where, full of strength and love,
   Hiram doth stand;
But if impostors are
Mixed with the worthy there,
Caution them to beware
   Of the right hand.

Now to the praise of those
Who triumphed o'er the foes
   Of Masons' arts:
To the praiseworthy three
Who founded this Degree,
May all their virtues be
   Deep in our hearts.

As they finish the second verse, each brother walks up in his turn to the Senior Warden, who stands behind a lattice-window, and thrusts his right hand, with the thumb and two first fingers open, and the third and little fingers clinched, palm up (see Fig. 22), through the hole in the window, receives his penny, withdraws his hand, and passes on, and so on until the candidate, who comes last, puts his hand through for his penny in this manner (see cut). The Senior Grand Warden seizes his hand, and, bracing his foot against the window, draws the candidate's

arm through to the shoulder, and exclaims vehemently, "An impostor! an impostor!" Another person exclaims, "Strike off his hand! strike off his hand!" and at the same time runs up with a drawn sword to give the blow. The Senior Deacon now intercedes for the candidate, and says: "Spare him! spare him! he is not an impostor; I know him to be a craftsman; I have wrought with him in the quarries."

S. G. W.—He is an impostor, for he has attempted to receive wages without being able to give the token, and the penalty must be inflicted.

S. D.—If you will release him, I will take him to our Right Worshipful Master, and state his case to him, and if the penalty must be inflicted, I will see it duly executed.

S. G. W.—On those conditions I will release him, provided he can satisfy me he is a Fellow Craft Mason.

The candidate now withdraws his arm, and gives the sign of a Fellow Craft Mason. (See Fig. 4, p. 17.)

The members of the Lodge then take their seats.

S. D. (taking candidate to Master).—Right Worshipful, this young craftsman has been detected as an impostor, at the office of the Senior Grand Warden, in attempting to receive wages, which were not his due, without being able to give the token.

R. W. M. (looking sternly at the candidate).—Are you a Fellow Craft Mason?

Candidate—I am. Try me.

R. W. M.—Give me the sign of a Fellow Craft Mason.

Candidate gives the sign of a Fellow Craft.

R. W. M. (to Senior Deacon).—It is well. He is undoubtedly a Fellow Craft. (Turning to candidate.) You have attempted to receive wages without being able to give the token. I am astonished that so intelligent-looking a young craftsman should thus attempt to impose upon us. Such conduct requires severe punishment. The penalty you have incurred is to have your right hand struck off. Have you ever been taught how to receive wages?

Candidate (prompted).—I have not.

R. W. M.—Ah, this in a measure serves to mitigate your crime. If you are instructed how to receive wages, will you do better for the future?

Candidate—I will.

R. W. M.—On account of your youth and inexperience, the penalty is remitted. Brother Senior Deacon, you will take this young craftsman, and give him a severe reprimand, and take him with you to the quarries, and there teach him how to bring up a regularly wrought stone.

The reprimand thus ordered to be given to the candidate is omitted in most Lodges at the present day, but, for the satisfaction of young Masons, and the curious, we insert it here.

S. D. (taking candidate by the collar.)—Young man, it appears you have come up here this evening to impose upon us; first, by presenting work which was not fit for the building, and then by claiming wages when there was not one farthing your due. Your work was not approved; you are not entitled to any wages, and had it not been for my timely interference, you would have lost your right hand, if not your life. Let this be a striking lesson to you, never to attempt to impose upon the craft hereafter. But go with me to the quarries, and there exhibit some specimens of your skill and industry; and if your work is approved, you shall be taught how to receive wages in a proper manner. Come, I say; go with me. (Shakes the candidate severely, and hurries him off into the preparation-room.)

The Senior Deacon returns to his seat in the Lodge, and the Junior Deacon prepares the candidate for the Degree, by divesting him of his outward apparel, and all money and valuables, his breast bare, and a cable-tow four times around his body; he is also securely blindfolded, with a hoodwink prepared for that purpose. In this condition he is conducted to the door by the Junior Deacon, who gives four distinct knocks. (● ● ● ●)

S. D.—Right Worshipful, while we are peaceably at work on the Fourth Degree in Masonry, the door of our Lodge appears to be alarmed.

R. W. M.—Brother Senior, attend to the cause of that alarm.

The Senior Deacon then steps to the door, and answers the alarm by four knocks. This is responded to from the outside by one knock, which is returned by the Senior Deacon. The door is then partly opened.

S. D.—Who comes there?

J. D.—A worthy brother, who has been regularly initiated as an Entered Apprentice Mason, served a proper time as such, passed to the Degree of a Fellow Craft, raised to the sublime Degree of a Master Mason, and now wishes for further light in Masonry, by being advanced to the honorary Degree of Mark Master Mason.

S. D.—Is it of his own free-will and accord he makes this request?

J. D.—It is.

S. D.—Is he duly and truly prepared?

J. D.—He is.

S. D.—Has he wrought in the quarries,[1] and exhibited specimens of his skill in the preceding Degrees?

J. D.—He has.

S. D.—By what further right or benefit does he expect this favor?

J. D.—By the benefit of a password.

S. D.—Has he a password?

J. D.—He has not; but I have it for him.

S. D.—Give it me.

Junior Deacon whispers in his ear the word JOPPA.

S. D.—The password is right. You will let him wait until the Right Worshipful Master is made acquainted with his request, and his answer returned.

Senior Deacon returns to the Right Worshipful Master, where the same questions are asked, and answers returned, as at the door.

R. W. M.—Since he comes endowed with the necessary qualifications, let him enter, in the name of the Lord, and take heed on what he enters.

The door is then opened—the candidate enters.

---

[1] There can be no doubt that the quarries from whence the Masons received their materials were situated very near to the Temple. Mr. Prime visited one of these quarries, situated beneath the City of Jerusalem, in 1856, and thus speaks of it: "One thing to me is very manifest. There has been solid stone taken from this excavation sufficient to build the walls of Jerusalem and the Temple of Solomon. The size of many of the stones taken from here appears to be very great. I know of no place to which the stone can have been carried but to these works, and I know of no other quarries in the neighborhood from which the great stone of the walls would seem to have come. These two connected ideas impelled me strongly toward the belief that this was the ancient quarry whence the city was built; and when the magnitude of the excavation between the two opposing hills and of this cavern is considered, it is, to say the least of it, a difficult question to answer, what has become of the stone once here, on any other theory than that I have suggested."—*Tent-Life in the Holy Land*, p. 118.

Another modern traveller, speaking of this quarry, says: "I have penetrated it for nearly half a mile, and seen there many large stones already cut, which were prepared for work but never removed. This new discovery is one of the greatest wonders of Jerusalem. It seems to extend under the Temple itself, and the stones were all finished and dressed there, and then raised up at the very spot for their appropriation."—*Christian Witness*, September 11, 1857.

S. D. (approaching candidate with a mallet and engraving chisel in his hands).—Brother, it becomes my duty to place a mark upon you which you will probably carry to your grave. As an Entered Apprentice, you were received upon one point of the compa·ses, pressing your naked left breast; as a Fellow Craft Mason, you were received upon the angle of a square, pressing your naked right breast; as a Master Mason, you were received upon both points of the compasses, extending from your naked left to the right breast. They were then explained to you. The chisel and mallet (placing the edge of the chisel against his breast) are instruments used by operative masons to hew, cut, carve, and indent their work; but we, as Free and Accepted Masons, make use of them for a more noble and glorious purpose. We use them to hew, cut, carve, and indent the mind. And, as a Mark Master Mason, we receive you upon the edge of the indenting chisel, and under the pressure of the mallet.

As he pronounces the last words, he braces his feet, raises his mallet, makes two or three false motions, and gives a violent blow upon the head of the chisel; throws down mallet and chisel, takes hold of the candidate's left arm.[1]

"Follow me."

They walk four times round the Lodge, and each time, as he passes the stations of the Master, and Senior and Junior Grand Wardens, they each give one loud rap with their mallet. The Master, in the mean time, reads from a text-book the following passages of Scripture: (●)

"The stone which the builders refused is become the head stone of the corner."—*Psalm* CXVIII. 22. (● ●)

Did ye never read in the Scriptures, "The stone which the builders rejected is become the head of the corner"?—*Gospel of St. Matthew* XXI. 42. (● ● ●)

And have you not read this Scripture, "The stone which the builders rejected is become the head of the corner"?—*Mark* XII. 10. (● ● ● ●)

What is this, then, that is written, "The stone which the builders rejected is become the head of the corner"?—*Luke* XX. 17.

The reading is so timed as to be completed just as the candidate arrives at the Junior Warden's post, who gives an alarm of four knocks, and the same questions are asked, and answers returned, as at the door.

The Junior Grand Warden directs him to his Senior, who, on

---

[1] The hoodwink is raised from over the candidate's eyes while this scene is being enacted, after which it is replaced again, and he is marched around the room four times.

his arrival, gives four raps, and the like questions are asked and answered. From thence he is directed to the Right Worshipful Master in the east, where the same questions are asked and the same answers are given. The Master then orders that the candidate be conducted back to the Senior Warden in the west, and be taught by him to approach the east by four upright, regular steps, his feet forming a square, and body erect at the altar. The candidate then kneels, and receives the obligation, as follows:—

I, Peter Gabe, of my own free-will and accord, in the presence of Almighty God, and this Right Worshipful Lodge of Mark Master Masons, erected to him and dedicated to Hiram the Builder, do hereby and hereon, in addition to my former obligations, most solemnly and sincerely promise and swear, that I will not give the secrets of a Mark Master Mason to any one of an inferior degree, nor to any other person in the known world, except it be a true and lawful brother, or brethren, of this degree; and not unto him nor unto them whom I shall hear so to be, but unto him and them only whom I shall find so to be, after strict trial and due examination, or lawful information given. Furthermore do I promise and swear, that I will support the Constitution of the General Grand Royal Arch Chapter of the United States of America, also the Grand Royal Arch Chapter of this State, under which this Lodge is held, and conform to all the by-laws, rules, and regulations of this or any other Lodge of Mark Master Masons, of which I may at any time hereafter become a member. Furthermore do I promise and swear, that I will obey all regular signs and summonses given, handed, sent, or thrown to me from the hand of a brother Mark Master Mason, or from the body of a just and legally constituted Lodge of such, provided it be within the length of my cable-tow. Furthermore do I promise and swear, that I will not wrong this Lodge, or a brother of this Degree, to the value of his wages (or one penny), myself, knowingly, nor suffer it to be done by others, if in my power to prevent it. Furthermore do I promise and swear, that I will not sell, swap, barter, or exchange my mark, which I shall hereafter choose, after it has been recorded in the book of marks, for any other one, unless it be a dead mark, or one of an older date, nor will I pledge it a second time until it is lawfully redeemed from the first pledge. Furthermore do I promise and swear, that I will receive a brother's mark when offered to me requesting a favor, and grant him his request if in my power; and if it is not in my power to grant his request, I will return him his mark with the value thereof, which is half a shekel of silver, or quarter of a dollar. To all of which I do most solemnly and sincerely promise and swear, with a fixed and steady purpose of mind in me to keep and perform the same, binding myself under no less penalty than to have my right ear smitten off, that I may forever be unable to hear the word, and my right hand chopped off, as the penalty of an impostor, if I should ever prove wilfully guilty of violating any part of this my solemn oath, or obligation, of a Mark Master Mason. So help me God, and make me steadfast to keep and perform the same.

R. W. M.—Detach your hand and kiss the book four times.

As soon as the candidate has taken the obligation, some brother makes an alarm on the outside of the door.

J. D. (rising.)—There is an alarm at the door, Right Worshipful.

R. W. M.—Attend to the alarm, brother, and see who comes there.

Junior Deacon inquires the cause of the alarm, and returns with a letter for the Right Worshipful Master, who opens it and reads as follows, or something to this effect:—

TO THE RIGHT WORSHIPFUL MASTER ST. JOHN'S MARK LODGE:

DEAR BROTHER—I am at present in a position where the possession of twenty-five dollars will greatly benefit me. Will you please see Brother Gabe, and ask him if he will loan me that amount? I regret to say that the only security I can offer for the loan is my *mark*, which I pledge until I refund him the money. Please see that he gets it, and send the money per the bearer.

Yours, fraternally,
JOHN JAY.

R. W. M. (to candidate, at the same time handing him the mark.)—Well, can you accommodate Brother Jay with this money he asks the loan of?

Candidate receives the mark, says he has no money about him; he cannot grant the request.

S. G. W.—Right Worshipful, I can accommodate Brother Jay with twenty-five dollars, if he will leave his mark with me as a pledge.

R. W. M. (to candidate).—Will you return the mark, then?

Candidate hands it back.

R. W. M.—How is this? Do you return it without the price, and thus break your oath before you rise from the altar? Have you not sworn, that where you could not grant a brother's request you would return his mark, with the price thereof, viz.: half a Jewish shekel of silver, or the fourth of a dollar?

Candidate is generally embarrassed, and replies that all his money was taken from him in the preparation-room.

R. W. M.—Are you sure that you have not even a quarter-dollar about you?

Candidate—I am.

R. W. M.—Look further. Perhaps some good friend has, in pity to your destitute situation, supplied you with that amount, unknown to yourself: feel in all your pockets, and if you find, after a thorough search, that you have really none, we shall have less reason to think that you meant willfully to violate your obligation.

The candidate feels in his pocket and finds a quarter of a dollar, which some brother had slyly placed there. He protests he had no intention of concealing it —really supposed he had none about him, and hands it to the Master, with the mark.

R. W. M.—Brother, let this scene be a striking lesson to you: should you ever hereafter have a mark presented you by a worthy brother, asking a favor, before you deny him make diligent search, and be quite sure of your inability to serve him; perhaps you will then find, as in the present instance, that some unknown person has befriended you, and you are really in a better situation than you thought yourself.[1]

The above is a true description of the manner in which the candidate was formerly taught his duty as a Mark Master Mason. In these *latter* days, however, very few Masters countenance this method of instruction, and it is therefore almost entirely discarded. The plan now generally adopted is as follows:—

After the candidate has taken the obligation, and while he is yet kneeling at the altar, the Right Worshipful Master presents him with a small metal mark (usually gold or silver), and requests the loan of a small sum of money upon it. The candidate takes the mark, but upon examination he finds that he has no money, all having been taken from him in the ante-room. He then attempts to give it back to the Right Worshipful Master, but the latter refuses to receive it, saying to the candidate:

I cannot, brother Gabe (or as the case may be), take it back:

---

[1] MARK.—It is a plate of gold or silver worn by Mark Masters. The form is generally that of a Mark Master's keystone, within the circular inscription there being engraved a device selected by the owner. This mark, on being adopted by a Mark Master, is recorded in the Book of Marks, and it is not lawful for him ever afterward to exchange it for any other. It is a peculiar pledge of friendship, and *its presentation by a destitute brother to another Mark Master, claims from the latter certain offices of friendship and hospitality, which are of solemn obligation among the brethren of this Degree.*—*Lexicon.*

were I to do so, I would violate my oath as a Mark Master, and so would you.

Here the Right Worshipful Master calls the candidate's attention to that part of the obligation.

The Right Worshipful Master now requests one of the brethren present to let the newly made brother Mark Master have the price of the Mark (usually twenty-five cents). Some brother here hands the candidate that sum, and he in turn hands it, together with the Mark, to the Right Worshipful Master. The Right Worshipful Master then administers the caution to candidate, beginning as follows:—

Brother, let this scene, &c. (See line 16, page 168.)

The Right Worshipful Master now takes the candidate by the hand, and says:

Arise, brother, and I will invest you with the pass-grip and word, and also the real grip and word of a Mark Master Mason.

The pass-grip of this Degree is made by extending the right arms and clasping the fingers of the right hands, as one would naturally do to assist another up a steep ascent. It is said to have originated from the fact that the banks of the river at Joppa were

FIG. 23

PASS-GRIP OF A MARK MASTER MASON

so steep that the workmen on the Temple had to assist each other up them while conveying the timber from the forests of Lebanon. The pass-word is JOPPA.[1]

FIG. 24

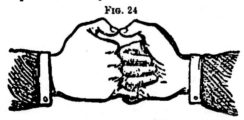

REAL GRIP OF A MARK MASTER MASON

[1] Yesterday morning at daybreak, boats put off and surrounded the vessel to take us to the town (JOPPA), the access to which is difficult, on account of the numerous

R. W. M. (to candidate).—Will you be *off*, or *from?*

Candidate (prompted).—From.

R. W. M.—From what?

Candidate—From the pass-grip to the true grip of a Mark Master Mason.

R. W. M.—Pass on.

The grip is made by locking the little fingers of the right hands, turning the backs of them together, and placing the ends of the thumbs against each other; its name is SIROC, or MARK WELL, and, when properly made, forms the initials of those two words: Mark well.

The Right Worshipful Master, after admonishing the candidate never to give the words in any way but that in which he received them, resumes his seat, when the brethren shuffle about their feet.

R. W. M.—What means this disturbance among the workmen, Brother Senior?

S. G. W. (rising).—Right Worshipful, the workmen are at a stand for the want of a certain keystone to one of the principal arches, which no one has had orders to make.

R. W. M.—A keystone to one of the principal arches? I gave our Grand Master, Hiram Abiff, strict orders to make that keystone, previous to his assassination. (Gives two raps with his gavel, which brings the three Overseers before him.) Brother Overseers, has there been a stone of this description brought up for inspection? (Exhibiting the figure of a keystone.)

Master Overseers—There was a stone of that description brought up for inspection, but it being neither oblong nor square, nor having the mark of any of the craft upon it, and we not knowing the mark that was upon it, supposed it unfit for the building, and it was thrown over among the rubbish.

R. W. M.—Let immediate search be made for it; the Temple cannot be finished without it; it is one of the most valuable stones in the whole building. (The brethren then shuffle about the Lodge again, and find the keystone, and bring it up to the east.)

rocks that present to view their bare flanks. The walls were covered with spectators, attracted by curiosity. The boats being much lower than the bridge, *upon which one is obliged to climb,* and having no ladder, *the landing is not effected without danger.* More than once it has happened, that passengers in springing out have broken their limbs, and we might have met with the like accident *if several persons had not hastened to our assistance.*—*Lexicon.*

There is an old tradition among Masons, that the banks of the river at Joppa were so steep as to render it necessary for the workmen to assist each other up by means of a *peculiar locking of the right hand,* which is still preserved in the Mark Master's Degree.—*Historical Landmarks,* vol. I. p. 426.

The Senior Warden takes the stone from the hands of the brethren, and then reports to the Right Worshipful Master as follows:—

Right Worshipful Master, the stone has been found; it was discovered buried in the rubbish of the Temple, and I herewith transmit it to you, by trusty brothers. (Two or three of the brethren carry it to the Right Worshipful Master in the east.

The Right Worshipful Master receives the keystone and places it in front of him, on the desk, upright and plumb, with the initials on it facing the whole Lodge, but more especially the candidate, who is seated in a chair in front of the Right Worshipful Master.[1]

The Right Worshipful Master gives four raps with the gavel (● ● ● ●), when all rise to their feet. (Some Lodges do not do so, but keep their seats.) When he reads the following passages of Scripture, at the end of each passage he strikes the keystone on the top with his gavel—first, one rap; second, two raps; and so on to the fourth passage, viz.:

Right Worshipful Master strikes the keystone once. (●)

"The stone which the builders refused is become the head stone of the corner."—*Ps.* CXVIII. 22.

Right Worshipful Master strikes the keystone twice. (● ●)

Did ye never read in the Scriptures, "The stone which the builders rejected is become the head of the corner"?—*Matt.* XXI. 42.

Right Worshipful Master strikes the keystone thrice. (● ● ●)

And have you not read this Scripture, "The stone which the builders rejected is become the head of the corner"?—*Mark* XII. 10.

Right Worshipful Master strikes the keystone four times. (● ● ● ●)

What is this, then, that is written, "The stone which the builders rejected is become the head of the corner"?—*Luke* XX. 17.

Master reads to candidate from text-book: "To him that overcometh will I give to eat of the hidden manna, and I will give him a white stone, and in the stone a new name written, which no man knoweth, saving him that receiveth it." (*Rev.* XI. 17.) Come forward, and receive the new name.

Candidate steps forward.

Master—Brother? I will now invest you with the new name that

---

[1] Some Lodges here call the candidate's attention to the indenting chisel and mallet, before reading the Scripture relative to the stone.

none but a Mark Master can receive. It is a circle of letters
which are the general mark of this Degree.

Here the Right Worshipful Master calls the candidate's attention
to the keystone before him, by pointing out to him the initials on
the stone, which he is informed read as follows:—

HIRAM, TYRIAN, WIDOW'S SON, SENDETH TO KING SOLOMON

The candidate is here instructed how to read the words when
challenged by any stranger, which is as follows:—
R. W. M.—Hiram.
Candidate—Tyrian.
R. W. M.—Widow's.
Candidate—Son.
R. W. M.—Sendeth.
Candidate—To.
R. W. M.—King.
Candidate—Solomon.
R. W. M. (pointing to the centre within the circle of these letters).
—Within this circle of letters every Mark Master Mason must
place his own private mark, which may be any device he may
choose to select; and when you have selected your mark, and it
is once regularly recorded in the Book of Marks of this or any
other Lodge of which you may be chosen a member, you have no
more right to change it than you have to change your own name.

Marks are not generally recorded; this duty is very much neg-
lected—it should be done, and strictly enforced in every Lodge.

Master reads to candidate: "He that hath an ear to hear, let
him hear."—*Rev.* III. 13.

The Master further instructs the candidate in the signs of the
penalties of this Degree (see Figs. 19, 20, 21, and 22), and then
presents, or points out to him on the chart, the working-tools of
a Mark Master Mason, viz.: a *mallet* and *chisel,* the use of which
he explains as follows:—

The *chisel* morally demonstrates the advantages of discipline
and education. The mind, like the diamond in its original state,

is rude and unpolished, but as the effect of the chisel on the external coat soon presents to view the latent beauties of the diamond, so education discovers the latent beauties of the mind, and draws them forth to range the large field of matter and space, to display the summit of human knowledge, our duty to God and

TOOLS OF A MARK MASTER

man. The *mallet* morally teaches to correct irregularities, and to reduce man to a proper level; so that by quiet deportment he may, in the school of discipline, learn to be content. What the mallet is to the workman, enlightened reason is to the passions: it curbs ambition, it depresses envy, it moderates anger, and it encourages good dispositions, whence arises among good Masons that comely order,

> "Which nothing earthly gives, or can destroy,
> The soul's calm sunshine, and the heartfelt joy."

R. W. M. (to candidate).—Brother, in taking this Degree, you have represented one of the Fellow Craft Masons who wrought at the building of King Solomon's Temple. It was their custom on the eve of the sixth day of the week to carry up their work for inspection. This young craftsman discovered in the quarries the keystone to one of the principal arches that had been wrought by the Grand Master, Hiram Abiff, and, throwing away his own work, he took it up to the Temple, where it was inspected by the Overseers, rejected as of no account, and thrown over among the rubbish. He then repaired to the office of the Senior Grand Warden to receive his wages; but not being able to give the token, he was detected as an impostor, which like to have cost him his right hand; but King Solomon pardoned him, and after a severe reprimand he was taken back to the quarries. Previous to the completion of the Temple, the progress of the work was interrupted for want of the keystone, which circumstance being communicated to King Solomon, he gave orders that search should be made for it among the rubbish, where it was found, and afterward applied to its intended use.

On the sixth hour of the sixth day of every week, the craft, being eighty thousand in number, formed in procession, and repaired to the office of the Senior Grand Wardens, to receive their wages; and in order to prevent the craft being imposed upon by unskilful workmen, each craftsman claiming wages was made to thrust his hand through a lattice window, and at the same time give this token, holding under the two last fingers of his hand a copy of his mark. (See Fig. 22, p. 156.)

The Senior Grand Warden casts his eye upon the corresponding mark in the book (where all the marks of the craft, eighty thousand in number, were recorded), and, seeing how much money was due to that particular mark, placed it between the thumb and two fore-fingers of the craftsman, who withdrew his hand and passed on; and so on, each in his turn, until all were paid off. If any person attempted to receive wages without being able to give the token, the Senior Grand Warden seized him by the hand, drew his arm through the window, held him fast, and exclaimed immediately, "An impostor!" Upon this signal, an officer, who was stationed there for that purpose, would immediately strike his arm off.

The following charge is then given to the candidate by the Right Worshipful Master:

Brother, I congratulate you on having been thought worthy of being advanced to this honorable Degree of Masonry. Permit me to impress it on your mind, that your assiduity should ever be commensurate with your duties, which become more and more extensive as you advance in Masonry. In the honorable character of Mark Master Mason, it is more particularly your duty to endeavor to let your conduct in the Lodge and among your brethren be such as may stand the test of the Grand Overseer's square; that you may not, like the unfinished and imperfect work of the negligent and unfaithful of former times, be rejected and thrown aside, as unfit for that spiritual building, that house not made with hands, eternal in the heavens. While such is your conduct should misfortunes assail you, should friends forsake you, should envy traduce your good name, and malice persecute you, yet may you have confidence that among Mark Master Masons you will find friends who will administer to your distresses, and comfort your afflictions: ever bearing in mind, as a consolation under the frowns of fortune, and as an encouragement to hope for better prospects, that the stone which the builders rejected, possessing merits to them unknown, became the chief stone of the corner.

The brethren shuffle round the Lodge again, as before.

R. W. M. (giving one rap).—Brother Senior, what is the cause of this disturbance?

S. G. W.—Right Worshipful, it is the sixth hour of the sixth day of the week, and the crafts are impatient to receive their wages.

R. W. M.—You will form them in procession, and let them repair to the office of the Senior Grand Warden and receive their wages.

Members form two and two and march around the Lodge against the sun, and sing from the text-book the last three verses of the Mark Master's Song. The Ceremony of paying the wages is gone through at the Master's seat in the east, the Master acting as Senior Grand Warden, and paying "every man a penny."

The members then inquire, each of the other, "How much have you?" The answer is given, "A penny." Some one asks the candidate the question, and he replies, "A penny." At this information, all the brethren pretend to be in a great rage, and hurl their pennies on the floor with violence, each protesting against the manner of paying the craft.

R. W. M. (giving one rap).—Brethren, what is the cause of this confusion?

S. D.—The craft are dissatisfied with the manner in which you pay them. Here is a young craftsman, who has just passed the square, and has received as much as we, who have borne the burden and fatigue of the day; and we don't think it is right and just, and we will not put up with it.

R. W. M.—This is the law, and it is perfectly right.

J. D.—I don't know of any law that will justify any such proceeding. If there is any such law, I should be glad if you would show it.

R. W. M.—If you will be patient, you shall hear the law. (Reads.) "For the kingdom of heaven is like unto a man that is an householder, which went out early in the morning, to hire laborers into his vineyard. And when he had agreed with the laborers for a penny a day, he sent them into his vineyard. And he went out about the third hour, and saw others standing idle in the market-place, and said unto them, Go ye also into the vineyard; and whatsoever is right, I will give you. And they went their way. And he again went out, about the sixth and ninth hour, and did likewise; and about the eleventh hour, he went out and found others standing idle, and saith unto them, Why stand ye here all the day idle? They say unto him, Because no man hath hired us. He saith unto them, Go ye also into the vineyard, and whatsoever is right, that shall ye receive. So when even was come, the lord of the vineyard saith unto his steward, Call the laborers, and give them their hire, beginning from the last unto the first. And when they came that were hired about the eleventh hour, they received every man a penny. But when the first came, they supposed that they should have received more; and they likewise received every man a penny. And when they had received it, they murmured against the good man of the house, saying, These last have wrought but one hour, and thou hast made them equal unto us, which have borne the burden and heat of the day. But he answered one of them, and said, Friend, I do thee no wrong: didst thou not agree with me for a penny? Take that thine is, and go thy way: I will give unto this last, even as unto thee. Is it not lawful for me to do what I will with my own? Is thine eye evil, because I am good? So the last shall be first, and the first last; for many are called, but few chosen."— *Matthew* xx. 1 to 16.

R. W. M.—Are you content?

Brethren (picking up their pennies).—We are satisfied.

LECTURE ON THE FOURTH, OR MARK MASTER'S DEGREE —
SECTION FIRST

Question. Are you a Mark Master Mason?

Answer. I am; try me.

Q. How will you be tried?

A. By the chisel and mallet.

Q. Why by the chisel and mallet?

A. Because they are the proper Masonic implements of this degree.

Q. Where were you advanced to the degree of Mark Master Mason?

A. In a regular and duly constituted Lodge of Mark Master Masons.

Q. What were the preparatory circumstances attending your advancement to this degree?

A. I was caused to represent one of the fellow crafts employed at the building of King Solomon's Temple, whose custom it was, on the eve of the sixth day of each week, to carry up their work for inspection.

Q. By whom was it inspected?

A. By three Overseers appointed by King Solomon, and stationed at the South, West, and East gates.

Q. How many fellow crafts were employed at the building of King Solomon's Temple?

A. Eighty fellow crafts.

Q. Among so large a number was not our Grand Master liable to be imposed upon by unskillful workmen presenting work unfit for use?

A. They were not, for King Solomon took the precaution that each craftsman should choose for himself a mark, and place it upon his work, so it should be readily known and distinguished when brought up promiscuously for inspection.

Q. What were the wages of a fellow craft whose work had been approved?

A. One penny a day.

Q. Among so large a number was not our Grand Master liable to be imposed upon by unskillful workmen demanding wages not their due?

A. They were not, for King Solomon took the further precaution that each craftsman demanding wages should thrust his right hand into the apartments of the Senior Grand Warden, with a copy of his mark in the palm thereof, at the same time giving this token (see page 156).

Q. To what does this token allude?

A. To the way and manner in which each fellow craft received his wages.

Q. Of what further use is it?

A. To distinguish a true craftsman from an impostor.

Q. When an impostor is discovered, what should be his penalty?

A. To have his right hand chopped off.

SECOND SECTION

Q. Where were you prepared to be advanced to the degree of Mark Master Mason?

A. In a room adjoining a regularly and duly constituted Lodge of Mark Master Masons.

Q. How were you prepared?

A. I was deprived of all metals, divested of my outward apparel, in a working posture, with a cable-tow four times around my body, in which situation I was conducted to the door of the Lodge, where a regular demand was made by four (4) distinct knocks.

Q. To what do the four (4) distinct knocks allude?

A. To the fourth (4th) degree of Masonry, it being that upon which I was about to enter.

Q. What was said to you from within?

A. Who comes here.

Q. Your answer?

A. A worthy brother who has been duly initiated, passed the degree of Fellow Craft, raised to the sublime degree of Master Mason, and now wishes for further promotion in Masonry by being advanced to the degree of Mark Master Mason.

Q. What were you then asked?

A. If it was an act of my own free will and accord, and if I was worthy and well qualified, duly and truly prepared; if I had wrought in the quarries and exhibited suitable specimens of skill in the preceding degree, and was properly vouched for; all of which being answered in the affirmative, I was then asked by what further right or benefit I expected to gain this important privilege.

Q. Your answer?

A. By the benefit of the pass.

Q. Give the pass. (Joppa!)

Q. To what does it allude?

A. To the ancient city of Joppa, where the materials for the Temple were landed when brought down from Mount Lebanon. Masonic tradition informs us that the sea-coast at that place was so nearly perpendicular it was difficult for workmen to ascend without the assistance from above, which assistance was afforded them, given by guards stationed there for that purpose. It has since been adopted as a proper pass to be given before gaining admission to any regular and well governed Lodge of Mark Master Masons.

Q. What was then said to you?

A. I was directed to wait until the Right Worshipful Master could be informed of my request, and his answer returned.

Q. What was his answer?

A. Let the candidate enter and be received in due and ancient form.

Q. How were you received?

A. On the edge of the engraver's chisel, applied to my naked left breast, and under the impression of the mallet, which was to teach that the moral precepts of this degree should make a deep and lasting impression upon my mind and future conduct.

Q. How were you then disposed of?

A. I was conducted four (4) times regularly around the Lodge to the Worshipful Junior Warden in the South, where the same questions were asked and answers returned as at the door.

Q. How did the Worshipful Junior Warden dispose of you?

A. He directed me to be conducted to the Worshipful Senior Warden in the West, where the same questions were asked and answers returned as before.

Q. How did the Worshipful Senior Warden dispose of you?

A. He directed me to be conducted to the Right Worshipful Master in the East, where the same questions were asked and answers returned as before.

Q. How did the Right Worshipful Master dispose of you?

A. He ordered me to be re-conducted to the Worshipful Senior Warden in the West, who taught me to approach to the East, advancing by four (4) upright regular Masonic steps, my feet forming a square and my body erect, to the Right Worshipful Master.

Q. How did the Right Worshipful Master dispose of you?

A. He made me a Mark Master Mason.

Q. How?

A. In due form?

Q. What is that due form?

A. Kneeling upon both knees, both hands covering the Holy Bible, square and compasses, in which due form I took upon myself the solemn oath or obligation of a Mark Master Mason.

Q. Have you that obligation?

A. I have.

Q. Will you give it?

A. I will, with your assistance.

Q. Proceed. I, A. B., &c., &c.

Q. Have you a sign in this degree?

A. I have several.

Q. Show me a sign? (Chopping off the right ear.)

Q. What is that called?

A. The dueguard.

Q. To what does it allude?

A. To the penalty of my obligation, that I should suffer my right ear to be smote off sooner than divulge any of the secrets of this degree unlawfully.

Q. Show me another sign? (Chopping off right hand.)

Q. What is that called?

A. The sign.

Q. To what does it allude?

A. To the additional portion of the penalty of my obligation, that I would sooner have my right hand striken off as the penalty of an impostor than divulge any of the secrets of this degree unlawfully.

Q. Show me another sign? (Carrying the key-stone.)

Q. What is that called?

A. The grand hailing sign of distress of a Mark Master Mason.

Q. To what does it allude?

A. To the way and manner each brother is obliged to carry his work while being advanced to this degree.

Q. Show me another sign? (Heave over.)

Q. What is that called?

A. The principal sign.

Q. To what does it allude?

A. To the principal words of this degree.

Q. What are they?

A. Heave over.

Q. To what does it further allude?

A. To the rejection of the "Key Stone" by the Overseers.

Q. How happened that circumstance?

A. Just before the completion of the Temple, our Grand Master, Hiram Abiff, was slain, as we have had an account in the preceding degree. It so happened on the eve of the sixth day of a certain week, when the craftsmen were bringing up their work for inspection, a young fellow craft seeing this piece of work, and concluding it designed for some portion of the Temple, brought it up.

Q. What followed?

A. On presenting it to the Junior Overseer at the south gate, he observed that it was neither a regular oblong nor a square, nor had it the mark of any of the workmen upon it; but, from its singular form and beauty, he was unwilling to reject it, and suffered it to pass to the Senior Overseer at the west gate.

Q. What followed?

A. He, for similar reasons, suffered it to pass to the Master Overseer at the east gate for his inspection.

Q. What followed?

A. The Master Overseer called together his brother Overseers and held a consultation, observing that it was neither a regular oblong nor a square; neither had it the mark of any of the workmen upon it; nor did they know that which was upon it, and concluding it unfit for use, agreed to heave it over among the rubbish.

Q. What followed?

A. The Senior Grand Warden informed King Solomon that the Temple was nearly completed, but the workmen were nearly at a stand for the want of a certain "key-stone," which none of them had had orders to furnish.

Q. What followed?

A. King Solomon observed that that particular piece of work had been assigned to one Grand Master Hiram Abiff; and, from his known skill and punctuality, he no doubt had completed it agreeable to the original design; ordered inquiry to be made of the Overseers, to see if any piece of work bearing a certain mark had been presented for inspection.

Q. What followed?

A. On inquiry being made it was found that there had; but it being neither a regular oblong nor a square, nor had it the mark of any of the workmen upon it; and they, not knowing that which was upon it, and concluding it unfit for use, agreed to heave it over among the rubbish.

Q. What followed?

A. King Solomon ordered strict search to be made in and about the several apartments of the Temple, and among the rubbish, to see if it could be found.

Q. What followed?

A. Search was accordingly made, the stone found, and afterwards applied to its intended use.

Q. Have you a grip to this degree?

A. I have several.

Q. Communicate it to me. (Give grip.)

Q. Has that a name?

A. It has.

Q. Give it? (Mark Well.)

Q. On what is this degree founded?

A. The key-stone to a certain arch in King Solomon's Temple.

Q. By whom was it wrought?

A. Our Grand Master, Hiram Abiff; but before he had given orders to have it carried up, he was slain, as we have had an account of it in the preceding degree.

Q. What was its color?

A. White; and to it alludes a certain passage of Scripture, which says: "To him that overcometh will I give to eat of the hidden manna, and I will give him a white stone, and in that stone a new name written, which no man knoweth save him that receiveth (or receives it).

Q. What is that new name?

A. It is composed of the words of which the letters on the "key-stone" are the initials.

Q. What are they?

A. "Hiram, Tyrian, Widow's, Son, Sendeth, To, King, Solomon."

Q. Of what use is this circle of letters?

A. It was the mark of our G. M., H. A.; it is now a general mark of this degree, in the centre of which each brother places his own private mark, to which the tie in the obligation particularly alludes.

Q. What is the price of a brother's mark?

A. A Jewish half shekel of silver, equal in value to one-quarter of a dollar.

Q. Were you, at any time during your advancement to this degree, called upon with this portion of your obligation?

A. I was.

Q. At what time?

A. While on my bended knees at the altar.

Q Why at that particular time?

A. To impress upon my mind in the most solemn manner that I should never hastily reject the application of a worthy brother, especially when accompanied by so sacred a pledge as his mark, but grant him his request if in my power; if not, return him his mark with the price thereof, which will enable him to procure the common necessaries of life.

Q. By whom was this degree founded?

A. Our three Grand Masters—Solomon King of Israel, Hiram King of Tyre, and Hiram Abiff.

Q. For what purpose was it founded?

A. To be conferred upon all those who should be found worthy and well qualified, not only as an honorary reward for their zeal, fidelity and attachment to Masonry, but to render it impossible that any brother who should be found worthy of being advanced to this degree should ever be reduced to such extreme indigence as to suffer for the common necessities of life, when the price of his mark would procure the same.

Q. Who does a brother represent, presenting a mark and receiving assistance?

A. Our Grand Master, Hiram Abiff, who was a poor man, but for his regular and upright deportment, his great skill in architecture and the sciences, became eminently distinguished among the craftsmen.

Q. Who does a brother represent, receiving a mark and granting assistance?

A. Our Grand Master, Solomon, King of Israel, who was a rich man and eminently distinguished for his great liberality.

Q. What are the working tools of a Mark Master Mason?

A. The chisel and mallet.

Q. What is the use of the chisel?

A. It is used by operative Masons to cut, carve, mark and engrave their work.

Q. What does it Masonically teach?

A. The chisel morally demonstrates the advantage of discipline and education. (See *Monitors, it is Monitorial.*)

Q. What is the use of the mallet?

A. It is used by operative Masons to knock off excrescences and smooth surfaces.

Q. What does it Masonically teach?

A. The mallet morally teaches to correct irregularities and to reduce man to a proper level, so that by quiet deportment he may, in the school of discipline, learn to be content. (See *Monitor, it is Monitorial.*)

PRAYER AT THE CLOSING OF A MARK MASTER'S LODGE

Supreme Grand Architect of the Universe, who sittest on the throne of mercy, deign to view our labors in the cause of virtue and humanity with the eye of compassion; purify our hearts, and cause us to know and serve thee aright. Guide us in the paths of rectitude and honor; correct our errors by the unerring square of thy wisdom, and enable us so to practise the precepts of Masonry, that all our actions may be acceptable in thy sight. So mote it be. Amen.[1]

[1] The legend of the Degree is in substance as follows: "A young Craftsman found in the quarries of Tyre a stone of peculiar form and beauty, which was *marked* with a double circle, containing certain mysterious characters that greatly excited his curiosity. He had the ambition to produce this stone to the inspecting Mark Master as a work of his own. But as it was neither a single nor a double cube, nor of any other prescribed form, it was rejected, notwithstanding the beauty of its execution, and cast forth among the rubbish. The young man then frankly told the Master that the work was not his own, but that he was induced to bring it up on account of its perfect workmanship, which he thought could not be equalled. Some time afterward, when one of the arches in the foundations of the Temple was nearly completed, the keystone was missing. It had been wrought in the quarries by H. A. B. *(Hiram Abiff)* himself, *and was marked with his mark.* Search was made for it in vain, when the adventure of the young Fellow Craft was recollected, and among the rubbish the identical stone was found, which completed the work."—*Historical Landmarks,* vol. II. p. 126.

MARK OF A MARK MASTER MASON

PAST MASTER, OR FIFTH DEGREE

THIS degree in Masonry was instituted to try the qualifications of a Master Mason before becoming Master of a Lodge, and no Mason can constitutionally preside over a Lodge of Master Masons unless he has been admitted to this Degree. A Mason usually takes this Degree before offering himself as a candidate for presiding in a Master's Lodge; but should it so happen that a Mason is elected Master of a Lodge who is not a Past Master, the Past Master's Degree may be conferred upon him without any other ceremony than that of administering the obligation. In such a case it is usually done by Royal Arch Masons, acting by order of a Grand Master.

The Past Master's Lodge consists of seven officers, as follows:—

1. Right Worshipful Master; 2. Senior Warden; 3. Junior Warden; 4. Secretary; 5. Treasurer; 6. Senior Deacon; 7. Junior Deacon.[1]

The interior arrangement is the same as in the first degree, and the officers are similarly seated. (See p. 8.)

---

[1] The regular officers of a Past Masters' Lodge correspond exactly with those of a Lodge of Master Masons.

The officers of a Chapter take rank in a Past Masters' Lodge as follows, viz.: the High Priest as Master; the King as Senior Grand Warden; the Scribe as Junior Grand Warden; the Treasurer and Secretary occupy the corresponding stations; the Principal Sojourner as Senior Deacon; the Royal Arch Captain as Junior Deacon, and the Tyler at his proper station.

The symbolic color of the Past Master's Degree is purple. The apron is of white lambskin, edged with purple, and should have the jewel of the Degree inscribed upon it. The collar is of purple, edged with gold. But, as Past Masters' Lodges are held under the warrants of Royal Arch Chapters, the collars, aprons, and jewels of the Chapter are generally made use of in conferring the Past Master's Degree.

When a Lodge of Past Masters is opened in due form, the ceremony is similar to that of a Master's Lodge. If there is a candidate in waiting he is usually introduced into the Lodge as though it were open on the Mark Master's Degree, and he is made a Past Master before he is aware of it. Since the many disclosures of this and other Degrees in Masonry, it requires a great deal of tact and ingenuity to confer this Degree so as to produce the effect desired. The candidate is elected to the Degree in the Royal Arch Chapter, as no business is permitted to be done in this Degree except that of initiation. Formerly it was the custom for all the members to wear their hats while conferring this Degree, but now no member wears his hat except the Right Worshipful Master. We will now proceed to give the manner of conferring this Degree "in old times," as described by Richardson, and, at the close, will give the reader an idea of the modern way of conferring it. By comparing this with Richardson's work, the initiated will perceive that we have made some trifling alterations, and corrected several errors which occur in that book.

A Master Mason wishing to enter on the Degree of Past Master, petitions the Chapter, and is balloted for in the same way that a candidate would be in one of the first Degrees; but he is received very differently. Having had the requisite ballot, the Junior Deacon conducts him into the Lodge, places him on a seat, and then repairs to his own station near the Senior Warden in the west. Soon after, a heavy alarm is given at the outer door.

J. D. (to the Master, rising).—There is an alarm at the outer door, Right Worshipful.

R. W. M.—Attend to the alarm, and see who comes there.

Junior Deacon goes to the door, and soon returns, bringing a letter to the Master, who opens it, and reads aloud to the Lodge as follows: —

DEAR BROTHER—Our dear mother has been taken suddenly very ill, and the physician despairs of saving her live. Come home immediately; do not lose a moment in delay.

Your affectionate sister,

ALICE.

R. W. M. (addressing the Lodge).—Brethren, you see by the
tenor of this letter to me that it is necessary I should leave immediately. You must appoint some one to fill the chair, for I
cannot stay to confer this Degree.

J. W.—Right Worshipful, I certainly sympathize with you for
the afflicting calamity which has befallen your family, and am
sorry that it seems so urgently necessary for you to leave; but
could you not stop a few moments? Brother Gabe has come on
purpose to receive this Degree, and expects to receive it. I believe he is in the room, and can speak for himself; and unless he
is willing to put off the ceremony, I do not see how you can avoid
staying.

The candidate, sympathizing with the Master, says he consents
to wait, and by no means desires the Right Worshipful to stay
one moment on his account.

J. W.—I thank our brother for his courtesy, but I have other
reasons, Right Worshipful, why I desire you should stay to confer
this Degree to-night. In the first place, it is uncertain when I
myself shall be able to attend again—then we might not get so
many brethren together at another meeting; and as this is a very
difficult Degree to confer, I feel that you ought to stay.

R. W. M.—Brethren, it is impossible for me to stay. You will
therefore appoint some one to fill the chair. There are a number
of brethren present who are well qualified to confer the degree;
you will therefore please to nominate.

J. W.—I nominate our Brother Senior Warden to fill the chair.

R. W M.—Brethren, it is moved and seconded that Brother
Senior Warden fill the chair this evening, to confer this Degree
on Brother Gabe. All those in favor will signify it by saying
aye. (Two or three of the members respond by saying aye.)
Those opposed will say no. (Nearly all the members exclaim,
No!) It is not a vote. Brethren will please nominate a new
Master.

S. W.—I nominate Brother Junior Warden to fill the chair.

The Master puts the question with a similar result, when some
member nominates Brother Gabe (the candidate), who is unan-
imously voted for and declared duly elected.

R. W. M.—Brother Gabe, you are elected Master of this Lodge.
Will you please to step this way and take the chair?

The candidate goes forward to take the chair, when the Right
Worshipful Master pushes him back, and says:

R. W. M.—Before you occupy the Master's chair, you must first
assent to the ancient regulations, and take an obligation to discharge with fidelity the duty of Master of the Lodge.

The candidate having no objection, the Master addresses him as follows:—

1. You agree to be a good man and true, and strictly to obey the moral law?

2. You agree to be a peaceful subject, and cheerfully to conform to the laws of the country in which you reside?

3. You promise not to be concerned in any plots or conspiracies against government; but patiently to submit to the dicisions of the supreme legislature?

4. You agree to pay a proper respect to the civil magistrates, to work diligently, live creditably, and act honorably by all men?

5. You agree to hold in veneration the original rules and patrons of Masonry, and their regular successors, supreme and subordinate, according to their stations, and to submit to the awards and resolutions of your brethren, when convened, in every case consistent with the Constitution of the Order?

6. You agree to avoid private piques and quarrels, and to guard against intemperance and excess?

7. You agree to be cautious in carriage and behavior, courteous to your brethren, and faithful to your Lodge?

8. You promise to respect genuine brethren, and discountenance impostors, and all dissenters from the original plan of Masonry?

9. You agree to promote the general good of society, to cultivate the social virtues, and to propagate the knowledge of the arts?

10. You promise to pay homage to the Grand Master for the time being, and to his office when duly installed, strictly to conform to every edict of the Grand Lodge, or general assembly of Masons, that is not subversive to the principles and groundwork of masonry?

11. You admit that it is not in the power of any man, or body of men to make innovations in the body of Masonry?

12. You promise a regular attendance on the committees and communications of the Grand Lodge, on receiving proper notice, and to pay attention to the duties of Masonry on all convenient occasions?

13. You admit that no new Lodge can be formed without permission of the Grand Lodge, and that no countenance be given to any irregular Lodge, or to any person clandestinely initiated therein, being contrary to the ancient charges of the Order?

14. You admit that no person can be regularly made a Mason in, or admitted a member of, any regular Lodge, without previous notice, and due inquiry into his character?

15. You agree that no visitors shall be received into your Lodge

without due examination, and producing proper vouchers of their having been initiated into a regular Lodge?

Do you submit to these charges, and promise to support these regulations, as Masters have done in all ages before you?

Candidate—I do.

R. W. M.—You will now take upon yourself the obligation of this Degree. Please to kneel at the altar.

The candidate is conducted to the altar, kneels on both knees, lays both hands on the Holy Bible, square, and compasses, and takes the following oath:

I, Peter Gabe, of my own free-will and accord, in presence of Almighty God, and this Worshipful Lodge of Past Master Masons, erected to him, and dedicated to the Holy Saints John, do hereby and hereon, most solemnly and sincerely promise and swear, in addition to my former obligations, that I will not give the secrets of a Past Master Mason, or any of the secrets pertaining thereto, to any one of an inferior Degree, nor to any person in the known world, except it be to a true and lawful brother, or brethren, Past Master Masons, or within the body of a just and lawfully constituted Lodge of such; and not unto him or unto them whom I shall hear so to be, but unto him and them only whom I shall find so to be, after strict trial and examination, or lawful information.

Furthermore do I promise and swear, that I will obey all regular signs and summonses sent, thrown, handed, or given from the hand of a brother of this Degree, or from the body of a just and lawfully constituted Lodge of Past Masters.

Furthermore do I promise and swear, that I will support the constitution of the General Grand Royal Arch Chapter of the United States; also, that of the Grand Chapter of the State in which this Lodge is located, and under which it is held, and conform to all the by-laws, rules, and regulations of this, or any other Lodge of which I may at any time become a member, so far as in my power.

Furthermore do I promise and swear, that I will not assist or be present at the conferring of this Degree upon any person who has not, to the best of my knowledge and belief, regularly received (in addition to the Degrees of Entered Apprentice, Fellow Craft, and Master Mason) the Degree of Mark Master, or been elected Master of a regular Lodge of Master Masons.

Furthermore do I promise and swear, that I will aid and assist all poor and indigent Past Master Masons, their widows and orphans, wherever dispersed around the globe, they applying to me as such, and I finding them worthy, so far as is in my power without material injury to myself or family.

Furthermore do I promise and swear, that the secrets of a brother of this Degree, delivered to me in charge as such, shall remain as secure and inviolable in my breast, as they were in his own before communicated to me, murder and treason excepted, and those left to my own election.

Furthermore do I promise and swear, that I will not wrong this Lodge, nor a brother of this Degree, to the value of one cent, knowingly, myself, nor suffer it to be done by others, if in my power to prevent it.

FIG. 25　　　　　　　　　　FIG. 26

DUEGARD AND STEP OF A PAST MASTER
SIGN OF A PAST MASTER

Furthermore do I promise and swear, that I will not govern this Lodge, or any other over which I may be called to preside, in a haughty and arbitrary manner; but will, at all times, use my utmost endeavors to preserve peace and harmony, among the brethren.

Furthermore do I promise and swear, that I will never open a

Lodge of Master Masons unless there be present three regular Master Masons, besides the Tyler; nor close the same without giving a lecture, or some section or part of a lecture, for the instruction of the Lodge.

Furthermore do I promise and swear, that I will not sit in a Lodge where the presiding officer has not taken the degree of Past Master Mason.

To all of which I do most solemnly and sincerely promise and swear, with a fixed and steady purpose of mind to keep and perform the same; binding myself under no less penalty than (in addition to all my former penalties) to have my tongue split from tip to root, that I might forever thereafter be unable to pronounce the word, should I ever prove wilfully guilty of violating any part of this my solemn oath, or obligation, of a Past Master Mason. So help me God, and make me steadfast to keep and perform the same.

FIG. 27

PAST MASTER'S GRIP

R. W. M. (to candidate).—Kiss the Book five times.

The obligation having been administered, the candidate rises, when the Master proceeds to give him the sign, word, and grip of this Degree, as follows:

R. W. M. (to candidate).—You now behold me approaching you from the east, under the step, sign, and duegard of a Past Master Mason.

The Master now steps off with his left foot, and then places the heel of his right foot at the toe of the left, so as to bring the two feet at right angles, and make them the right angle of a square. He then gives the sign, placing the thumb of his right hand (fingers clinched) upon his lips. It alludes to the penalty of having his tongue split from tip to root. (See Fig. 25, p. 189.)

The Master then gives a second sign by placing his right hand upon the left side of his neck, and drawing it edgewise downward toward the right side, so as to cross the three former penalties. (See Fig. 26, p. 189.)

R. W. M.—Brother, let me now have the pleasure of conducting you into the *oriental chair* of King Solomon. (Places a large cocked hat on his head, and seats him in a chair in front of the Master's chair.) That wise king, when old and decrepit, was attended by his two friends, Hiram, King of Tyre, and Hiram Abiff, who raised and seated him in his chair by means of the Past Master's grip. (See Fig. 27.)

The Master and Senior Warden now take the candidate by this grip, and raise him on his feet several times, each time letting him sit back in the chair again. The Senior Warden then goes back to his seat, the candidate rises, and the Right Worshipful Master instructs him in the grip and word of a Past Master Mason. They first take each other by the Master Mason's grip (see Fig. 17, p. 120), and, putting the insides of their feet together, the Master whispers GIBLEM[1] in the ear of the candidate. At that moment they slip their right hands so as to catch each other just above the wrist of the left arm, and raise their left hands, catching each other's right elbow, the Master saying, and the candidate repeating (in union with these motions), "From a grip to a span, from a span to a grip," afterward (almost at the same instant) letting the left hand slip up the right arm to the back of each other, the Master saying, "A threefold cord is strong," and the candidate (prompted) replying. "A fourfold cord is not easily broken." (See Fig. 27.)

The Right Worshipful Master seats the candidate in the Master's chair, places a hat on his head, and then comes down in front, and says:

Worshipful brother, I now present you with the furniture and various Masonic implements of our profession; they are emblematical of our conduct in life, and will now be enumerated and explained as presented.

The Holy Writings, that great light in Masonry, will guide you

---

[1] The Giblemites, or, as they are called in Scripture, the *Giblim*, were inhabitants of the city and district of Gebal, in Phœnicia, near Mount Lebanon, and were, therefore, under the dominion of the King of Tyre. The Phœnician word *"gibal,"* which makes *"giblim"* in the plural, signifies a mason or stone-squarer. In the Second Book of Kings, v. 17, 18, we read that "the King commanded, and they brought great stones, costly stones, and hewed stones, to lay the foundation of the house. And Solomon's builders and Hiram's builders did hew them, and the stone-squarers," which last word is, in the original, *giblim*. Gesenius says that the inhabitants of Gebal were seamen and builders, and Sir William Drummond asserts that "the Giblim were Master Masons, who put the finishing hand to Solomon's Temple." In this sense the word is also used in the Book of Constitutions, which records that John de Spoulee, who, as one of the deputies of Edward III., assisted in rebuilding Windsor Castle, was called the "Master of the Giblim." The Giblim, or the Giblimites, were, therefore, stone-squarers or Master Masons.—*Book of the Chapter*, p. 56.

to all truth; it will direct your path to the temple of happiness, and point out to you the whole duty of man.

The Square teaches to regulate our actions by rule and line, and to harmonize our conduct by the principles of morality and virtue.

The Compasses teach to limit our desires in every station; thus rising to eminence by merit, we may live respected and die regretted.

The Rule directs that we should punctually observe our duty, press forward in the path of virtue, and neither inclining to the right nor to the left, in all our actions have eternity in view.

The Line teaches the criterion of moral rectitude; to avoid dissimulation in conversation and action, and to direct our steps to the path that leads to immortality.

The Book of Constitutions you are to search at all times; cause it to be read in your Lodge, that none may pretend ignorance of the excellent precepts it enjoins.

Lastly, you receive in charge the By-laws of your Lodge, which you are to see carefully and punctually executed. I will also present you with the Mallet; it is an emblem of power. One stroke of the mallet calls to order, and calls up the Junior and Senior Deacons; two strokes call up all the subordinate officers; and three, the whole Lodge.

R. W. M.—Brethren, please to salute your new Master.

All the brethren present, headed by the Master, now walk in front of the chair, give the sign of an Entered Apprentice, and pass on. This is repeated, with the sign of each Degree in Masonry up to that of Past Master.

R. W. M. (to candidate).—I now leave you to the government of your Lodge. (Master takes his seat with the brethren.)

The Senior Warden now steps forward and delivers up his jewel and his gavel to the new Master, and each of the other officers of the Lodge does the same, taking his turn according to rank. Presently the retired Master rises.

Retired Master (addressing the Chair).—Right Worshipful, in consequence of my resignation, and the election of a new Master, the seats of the Wardens have become vacant. It is necessary you should have Wardens to assist you in the government of your Lodge. I presume the brethren who have held these stations will continue to serve, if you so request.

The new Master requests the Senior Warden to resume his jewel and gavel, when the other officers (who had left their places) also resume their seats.

Retired Master—Right Worshipful, I would respectfully suggest to you, that as the office of Treasurer is one of considerable responsibility—he holding all the funds and property of the Lodge —you should direct that he be nominated and elected by the members present. This has been customary, and if you order a nomination to be made in this manner, I have no doubt that we shall select some one who will be satisfactory to you.

Candidate (acting as Master).—The brethren will please nominate a Treasurer for this Lodge.

Here a scene of confusion takes place, which is not easily described. The newly installed Worshipful is made the butt for every worthy brother to exercise his wit upon. Half-a-dozen are up at a time, soliciting the Master to nominate them, urging their several claims, and decrying the merits of others with much zeal; crying out, "Order, Worshipful! keep order!" Others propose to dance, and request the Master to sing for them; others whistle, or sing, or jump about the room; or scuffle and knock down chairs or benches. One proposes to call from labor to refreshment; another makes a long speech, advocating the reduction of the price of the Chapter Degrees from twenty dollars to ten, and recommending that it be permitted to pay for them in flour, or any other produce. His motion is seconded, and the new Master is pressed on all sides to put the question. If the question is put, the brethren all vote against it, and accuse the new Master of breaking his oath, when he swore he would support the Constitution of the General Grand Royal Arch Chapter, which establishes the price of the four Chapter Degrees at twenty dollars. If the Master attempts to exercise the power of the gavel, it often has the contrary effect; for if he gives more than one rap, and calls to order, every one obeys the signal with the utmost promptness, and drops on the nearest seat. The next instant, before the Master can utter a word, all are on their feet again, and as noisy as ever. Some brother now proposes that the Lodge be closed; another one hopes it will be closed in a short way.

Retired Master (to candidate).—Right Worshipful, it is moved and seconded that this Lodge be closed. You can close it as you please. You can merely declare the Lodge closed, or in any other way.

The candidate, being much embarrassed, will often attempt to close the Lodge by rapping with his gavel, and declaring it closed. Should he do so, the retired Master stops him as follows:

Retired Master—Right Worshipful, you swore in your obligation, that you would not close this or any other Lodge over which you should be called to preside, without giving a lecture or some part thereof. Do you intend to break your oath?

Candidate—I had forgotten that in this confusion. I hope the brethren will excuse me.

A brother goes and whispers to the candidate, telling him that he can resign the chair to the old Master, and have him close the Lodge, if he so prefers. The candidate is very glad to do this, and cheerfully abdicates his seat.

R. W. M. (resuming the chair).—Brother, the lesson we have just given, notwithstanding its apparent confusion, is designed to convey to you, in a striking manner, the necessity of at all times abstaining from soliciting, or accepting any office or station that you do not know yourself amply qualified to fill.

The Master now delivers the lecture in this Degree. It is divided into five sections. The first treats of the manner of constituting a Lodge of Master Masons. The second treats of the ceremony of installation, including the manner of receiving candidates to this Degree, as given above. The third treats of the ceremonies observed at laying the foundation-stones of public structures. The fourth section, of the ceremony observed at the dedication of Masonic Halls. The fifth, of the ceremony observed at funerals, according to the ancient custom, with the service used on the occasion. The lecture is usually read from a Monitor, which is kept in every Lodge. (See Lecture, page 197.)

The foregoing includes all the ceremonies ever used in conferring the Degree of Past Master; but the ceremonies are frequently shortened by the omission of some part of them; the presenting of the various implements of the profession, and their explanations, are often dispensed with; and, still more often, the charge.

Such is the manner in which this Degree was formerly conferred; but, as we have previously said, the ceremonies are now much abridged. The method of initiation to this Degree now usually adopted is as follows: The candidate for the Degree of Past Master is invited into a Lodge of Mark Masters, and as soon as he is seated, some one of the brethren rises and moves that the Lodge be closed. Another brother immediately gets up and proceeds to call the Master's attention to some unfinished business or the report of some committee. This action is all a *ruse*, and only intended to mislead the candidate from their real design. He (the candidate) sits there, thinking all the while that he is witnessing the regular business of a Mark Lodge, whereas he is in reality passing the preliminary steps of initiation. One of the brethren now moves an adjournment, another rises and opposes the motion, while a third asks the Chapter to help him with a loan of money. Some one of the members will oppose the loan, and high words frequently pass between the brethren (all for effect). Finally, the Right Worshipful Master will attempt to put to vote some resolutions on the subject, and a lengthy debate ensues as to the legality of this disposition of the funds of the Chapter. After the debate has proceeded for some time, one of the brethren rises and accuses the Right Worshipful Master of corruption, and charges him in plain terms with being interested in obtaining the loan. Upon this the Right Worshipful Master indignantly repels the insinuation, and demands to be relieved from serving any longer as Master of the Lodge. Another scene of excitement then ensues—some of the brethren favor the removal of the Right Worshipful Master, while others advocate his retaining his position. Finally, the Right Worshipful Master refuses to serve under any consideration, and peremptorily resigns. Some of the members now urge the pretended late Right Worshipful Master to assist in instating his successor to office. This he consents to do. The candidate is then nominated, elected, and placed in the Oriental chair, etc. The balance of the Degree, from the election of the Master, is correct, as given by Richardson in the foregoing pages, only the candidate is very seldom treated so badly as is represented there. The candidate is usually relieved from embarrassment in good season by the retired Master, who resumes his seat and reads the following charge to him:—

BROTHER—The conferring at this time of a Degree which has no historical connection with the other capitular Degrees is an apparent anomaly, which, however, is indebted for its existence to the following circumstances:

Originally, when Royal Arch Masonry was under the government of symbolic Lodges, in which the Royal Arch Degree was then always conferred, it was a regulation that no one could receive it unless he had previously presided as the Master of that or some other Lodge; and this restriction was made because the Royal Arch was deemed too important a Degree to be conferred only on Master Masons.

But, as by confining the Royal Arch to those only who had been actually elected as the presiding officers of their Lodges, the extension of the Degree would have been materially circumscribed, and its usefulness greatly impaired, the Grand Master often granted, upon due petition, his dispensation to permit certain Master Masons (although not elected to preside over their Lodges) "to pass the chair," which was a technical term, intended to designate a brief ceremony, by which the candidate was invested with the mysteries of a Past Master, and, like him, entitled to advance in Masonry as far as the Royal Arch, or the perfection and consummation of the Third Degree.

When, however, the control of the Royal Arch was taken from the symbolic Lodges and intrusted to a distinct organization—

that, namely, of Chapters—the regulation continued to be observed, for it was doubtful to many whether it could legally be abolished; and, as the law still requires that the august Degree of Royal Arch shall be restricted to Past Masters, our candidates are made to pass the chair simply as a preparation and qualification toward being invested with the solemn instructions of the Royal Arch.

The ceremony of passing the chair, or making you in this manner a Past Master, does not, however, confer upon you any official rank outside of the Chapter, nor can you in a symbolic Lodge claim any peculiar privileges in consequence of your having received in the Chapter the investiture of the Past Master's Degree. Those who receive the Degree in symbolic Lodges as a part of the installation service, when elected to preside, have been properly called "Actual Past Masters," while those who pass through the ceremony in a Chapter, as simply preparatory to taking the Royal Arch, are distinguished as "Virtual Past Masters," to show that, with the investiture of the secrets, they have not received the rights and prerogatives of the Degree.

With this brief explanation of the reason why this Degree is now conferred upon you, and why you have been permitted to occupy the chair, you will retire, and suffer yourself to be prepared for those further and profounder researches into Masonry, which can only be consummated in the Royal Arch Degree.[1]

If there is no further business, the lecture is delivered by the Right Worshipful Master, and the Lodge closed with the following prayer:[2]

[1] See Mackey's "Book of the Chapter."
[2] The chief object of this Degree in the United States is to exemplify the necessity of government, and to enforce upon the minds of those who are called to govern, the importance of qualifying themselves for the skilful and efficient discharge of their duties. The ceremonies of the Degree extend to no great length; but they are such as strongly to impress upon the newly elected Master a sense of his own deficiencies in the matter of government, and the need he has of promptness and energy in preserving the discipline of the Society over which he is to preside. The process of conferring the Degree, teaching by practical illustration, is apparently grave, though withal rather amusing. After the Lodge is opened upon the Third Degree, the Master receives intelligence from without that some sudden emergency demands his presence in another place. He therefore resigns the chair, and desires the brethren to elect a successor. The new Master is placed in the chair; but from various causes, too long to be enumerated here, he finds himself utterly unable to keep order, when the old Master reappears and kindly relieves him from his embarrassment, by teaching him how to command obedience; for it frequently happens that, in the plenitude of his power, a scrupulous compliance with his own ignorant and inopportune mandates has occasioned the very confusion which had appalled him.—*Historical Landmarks,* vol. II. p. 128.

PAST MASTERS—An honorary Degree conferred on the W. *(Worshipful) Master,* at his installation into office. In this Degree, the necessary instructions are conferred

Supreme Architect of the Universe, accept our humble praises for the many mercies and blessings which Thy bounty has conferred on us, and especially for this friendly and social intercourse. Pardon, we beseech Thee, whatever Thou hast seen amiss in us since we have been together, and continue to us Thy presence, protection and blessing. Make us sensible of the renewed obligations we are under to love Thee supremely, and to be friendly to each other. May all our irregular passions be subdued, and may we daily increase in Faith, Hope, and Charity, but more especially in that Charity which is the bond of peace, and the perfection of every virtue. May we so practise Thy precepts that we may finally obtain Thy promises, and find an entrance through the gates into the temple and city of our God. So mote it be. Amen.

LECTURE ON THE FIFTH, OR PAST MASTER'S DEGREE.—PART OF THE SECOND SECTION [1]

Question. Are you a Past Master?
Answer. I have the honor so to be.
Q. How gained you this distinguished honor?
A. By having been regularly elected and duly installed to preside over and govern a Lodge of Free and Accepted Masons. Previous to my installation I was caused to kneel at the altar in due form, and take upon myself a solemn oath or obligation to keep and conceal the secrets belonging to the chair.
Q. What is that due form?
A. Kneeling upon both knees, both hands covering the Holy Bible, square and compasses, my body erect; in which due form I took upon myself the solemn oath or obligation of a Past Master.
Q. Have you that obligation?
A. I have.
Q. Will you give it?
A. I will, with your assistance.
Q. Proceed. I, A. B., &c., &c. (See obligation of a Past Master.)

respecting the various ceremonies of the Order, such as installations, processions, the laying of corner-stones, etc. The ceremonies of the Degree, when properly conferred, inculcate a lesson of diffidence in assuming the responsibilities of an office without a due preparation for the performance of its duties.—*Lexicon.*
[1] This portion of the second section of the Lecture on the Fifth Degree relates to the induction of candidates, and is not given in the Monitors. With the exception of this, the Lecture may be found in "Webb's Monitor."

Q. Have you a sign belonging to the Chair?

A. I have several.

Q. Show me a sign? (Give sign, thumb to mouth.)

Q. What is that called?

A. The duegard.

Q. To what does it allude?

A. To the penalty of my obligation, that I would sooner have my tongue cleave to the roof of my mouth, than divulge any of the secrets belonging to the chair unlawfully.

Q. Show me another sign? (Give sign, drop your hand in from mouth in a circular manner down over your breast to your right side.)

Q. What is that called?

A. The sign.

Q. To what does it allude?

A. To the additional portion of the penalty of my obligation, that I would sooner suffer the severest inflictions of all my former penalties, than divulge any of the secrets belonging to the chair unlawfully.

Q. Have you a grip belonging to the chair?

A. I have.

Q. Communicate it to a brother. (Give the Past Master's grip. See the grip.)

Q. Has it a name?

A. It has.

Q. Give it. (Give the word. See word of Past Master.)

Q. What does it signify?

A. Stone squarer.

Q. What were you presented with?

A. The jewel of my office—which is a square, and it was hoped I would prepare a square stone in the Temple of Masonry.

Q. What were you next presented with?

A. The three great lights in Masonry, the Holy Bible, square and compasses. Within that sacred volume I would find all that was necessary for my counsel and guidance, these three great lights I was always to see in proper position when the lodge was open. If in the E. A. degree, that both points of the compasses are beneath the square; if in the F. C. degree, one point is elevated above the square; if in the Master's degree, both points are elevated above the square.

Q. What were you next presented with?

A. The charter or warrant, which would empower me to do all regular Masonic work.

Q. What were you next presented with?

A. The constitution, which I was carefully to search, and see that it was not infringed.

Q. What were you next presented with?

A. The By-laws, which I was to carefully search and see that they were strictly enforced.

Q. What were you next presented with?

A. The records, which I was to see carefully kept, that nothing improper be transmitted to paper, and have a general supervision over the duties of the secretary.

Q. What were you next presented with?

A. I, as Master should be covered; [1] while the rest of the brethren remained uncovered.

Q. What were you next presented with?

A. Last, but not least, I was presented with the gavel, which I was informed was an emblem of power, one blow of which would call the Lodge to order; and in opening and closing, the deacons would arise; two blows would call up the rest of the subordinate officers, on three blows, the whole Lodge; one blow would again seat them and call the Lodge to order.

Q. How were you then disposed of?

A. I was conducted to the chair, once so ably filled by our Grand Master Solomon, King of Israel, and it was hoped that a portion of his wisdom would rest upon and abide with me.

Q. What are the duties of the chair?

A. They are many and various.

Q. Of what do they consist?

A. In opening, instructing and closing Lodges; of initiating, crafting, and raising Masons; presiding at consecrations, dedications and installations; at the laying of corner stones of public edifices; presiding at funeral obsequies, and all other duties corresponding thereunto and connected therewith.

[1] A hat.

PAST MASTER'S JEWEL

MOST EXCELLENT MASTER, OR SIXTH DEGREE

No Mason can receive the Degree of Most Excellent Master until after he has become a Past Master, and presided in a Lodge, or, in other words, been inducted into the Oriental Chair of King Solomon. When the Temple of Jerusalem was finished,[1] those who had proved themselves worthy, by their virtue, skill, and fidelity, were installed as Most Excellent Masters, and, even at this date, none but those who have a perfect knowledge of all preceding Degrees are (or should be) admitted.[2]

[1] The Masonic tradition upon which the Degree is founded is described in the ancient Book of Constitutions, in the following words:

"The Temple was finished, in the short space of seven years and six months, to the amazement of all the world; when the cope-stone was celebrated by the fraternity with great joy. But their joy was soon interrupted by the sudden death of their dear Master, Hiram Abiff, whom they decently interred in the Lodge near the Temple, according to ancient usage.

"After Hiram Abiff was mourned for, the tabernacle of Moses and its holy relics being lodged in the Temple, Solomon, in a general assembly, dedicated or consecrated it by solemn prayer and costly sacrifices past number, with the finest music, vocal and instrumental, praising Jehovah upon fixing the holy ark in its proper place, between the cherubim; when Jehovah filled his own Temple with a cloud of glory."

[2] It is an established doctrine of the Order, that while three form a Lodge, and five may hold it, seven only can make it perfect. In such a case there requires an intermediate Degree to complete the series; for the Mark and Past Masters have been already admitted into the Craft Lodges. This Degree, as used by our transatlantic brethren, who are zealous and intelligent Masons, is called the Excellent Master, and the routine is thus stated: 1. E. A. P.; 2. F. C.; 3. M. M.; 4. Mark Master;

A Lodge of Most Excellent Masters is opened in nearly the same manner as Lodges in the preceding Degrees. The officers are, a Master, Senior and Junior Wardens and Deacons, Secretary and Treasurer, and of course a Tyler.

The officers of a Chapter rank as follows:—

The High Priest, as Right Worshipful Master; King, as Senior Warden; Scribe, as Junior Warden; Principal Sojourner, as Senior Deacon; Royal Arch Captain, as Junior Deacon. The Treasurer, Secretary, and Tyler corresponding in rank with the same officers of other Degrees.

The symbolic color of the Most Excellent Master's Degree is purple. The apron is of white lambskin, edged with purple. The collar is of purple, edged with gold. But, as Lodges of this Degree are held under warrants of Royal Arch Chapters, the collars, aprons, and jewels of the Chapter are generally made use of in conferring the Degree.

The Right Worshipful Master represents King Solomon, and should be dressed in a crimson robe, wearing a crown, and holding a sceptre in his hand.

A candidate receiving this Degree is said to be "received and acknowledged as a Most Excellent Master."

Lodges of Most Excellent Masters are "dedicated to King Solomon."

The officers of the Lodge are stationed as in the Entered Apprentice's Degree, described on Page 8. The Master presiding calls the Lodge to order, and says:

Master (to the Junior Warden).—Brother Junior, are they all Most Excellent Masters in the south?

J. W.—They are, Right Worshipful.

Master (to the Senior Warden).—Brother Senior, are they all Most Excellent Masters in the west?

S. W.—They are, Right Worshipful.

Master—They are also in the east.

Master gives one rap, which calls up the two deacons.

Master (to Junior Deacon).—Brother Junior, the first care of a Mason?

J. D.—To see the door tyled, Most Excellent.

Master—Attend to that part of your duty, and inform the Tyler that we are about to open this Lodge of Most Excellent Masters, and direct him to tyle accordingly.

Junior Deacon goes to the door and gives six knocks, which the Tyler from without answers by six more. He then gives one knock, which the Tyler answers with one, and he then partly opens the door, and informs the Tyler that by order of the Most Excellent Master a Lodge of Most Excellent Masters is now about to be opened in this place, and he must tyle accordingly. He then returns to his place and addresses the Master:

J. D.—The Lodge is tyled, Most Excellent.

Master—By whom?

J. D.—By a Most Excellent Master Mason without the door, armed with the proper implements of his office.

Master—His duty there?

J. D.—To keep off all cowans and eavesdroppers, and see that none pass or repass without permission of the Right Worshipful Master.

The Master now questions each officer of the Lodge as to his duties, which are recited by them as in the other Degrees.

Master (to Senior Warden).—Brother Senior, you will assemble the brethren around the altar for our opening.

S. W.— Brethren, please to assemble around the altar, for the purpose of opening this Lodge of Most Excellent Master Masons.

The brethren now assemble around the altar, and form a circle, and stand in such a position as to touch each other, leaving a space for the Right Worshipful Master; they then all kneel on their left knee, and join hands, each giving his right-hand brother his left hand, and his left-hand brother his right hand; their left arms uppermost, and their heads inclining downward: all being thus situated, the Right Worshipful Master reads the following verses from Psalm XXIV:

"The earth is the Lord's, and the fulness thereof; the world, and they that dwell therein. For he hath founded it upon the seas, and established it upon the floods. Who shall ascend into the hill of the Lord? and who shall stand in his holy place? He that hath clean hands, and a pure heart: who hath not lifted up his soul unto vanity, nor sworn deceitfully. He shall receive the blessing from the Lord, and righteousness from the God of his salvation. This is the generation of them that seek him, that seek thy face, O Jacob. Selah. Lift up your heads, O ye gates (here the kneeling brethren alternately raise and bow their heads as the reading proceeds); and be ye lifted up, ye everlasting doors; and the King of glory shall come in. Who is this King of glory? The Lord, strong and mighty; the Lord, mighty in battle. Lift up your heads, O ye gates; even lift them up, ye everlasting doors; and the King of glory shall come in. Who is this King of glory? The Lord of hosts; he is the King of glory. Selah."

While reading these verses, the Right Worshipful Master advances toward the circle of kneeling brethren, taking his steps only when reading those passages relative to the King of glory.

The reading being ended the Right Worshipful Master then kneels, joins hands with the others, which closes the circle, and they all lift their hands, as joined together, up and down, six times, keeping time with the words as the Right Worshipful Master repeats them: "One, two, three; one, two, three." This is Masonically called balancing. They then rise, disengage their hands, and lift them up above their heads, with a moderate and somewhat graceful motion, and cast up their eyes; turning at the same time to the right, they extend their arms, and then suffer them to fall loose and somewhat nerveless by their sides. This sign is said by Masons, to represent the sign of astonishment made by the Queen of Sheba, on first viewing Solomon's Temple. (See Fig. 30.)

The Right Worshipful Master resumes his seat and says: "Brethren, attend to the signs." He himself then gives all the signs, from an Entered Apprentice up to this Degree, and the brethren join and imitate him.

Master (to the Senior Warden).—Brother Senior, it is my will and pleasure that this Lodge of Most Excellent Masters be now opened for dispatch of business, strictly forbidding all private committees, or profane language, whereby the harmony of the same may be interrupted, while engaged in their lawful pursuits, under no less penalty than the by-laws enjoin, or a majority of the brethren may see cause to inflict.

The Senior Warden repeats this to his Junior, and the Junior announces it to the Lodge, as follows:

J. W.—Brethren, you have heard our Right Worshipful Master's will and pleasure, as just communicated to me—so let it be done.

The Lodge being opened, the ordinary business of the evening in gone through with, as in the former Degrees. If a candidate is to be initiated, the Junior Deacon goes to the preparation-room, where he is in waiting, and prepares him. He takes off the candidate's coat, puts a cable-tow six times round his body, and conducts him to the door of the Lodge, where he gives six distinct knocks (which are answered by the Senior Deacon from within), and then one knock, which is answered in the same manner.

S. D. (partly opening the door).—Who comes there?

J. D.—A worthy brother, who has been regularly initiated as an Entered Apprentice Mason; passed to the Degree of Fellow Craft; raised to the sublime Degree of Master Mason; advanced to the honorary Degree of a Mark Master Mason; presided in the chair as Past Master; and now wishes for further light in Masonry, by being received and acknowledged as a most Excellent Master.

S. D.—Is it of his own free-will and accord he makes this request?

J. D.—It is.

S. D.—Is he duly and truly prepared?

J. D.—He is.

S. D.—Is he worthy and well qualified?

J. D.- He is.

S. D.—Has he made suitable proficiency in the preceding Degrees?

J. D.—He has.

S. D.—By what further right or benefit does he expect to obtain this favor?

J. D.—By the benefit of a pass-word.

S. D.—Has he a pass-word?

J. D.—He has it not; but I have it for him.

S. D.—Give it to me.

Junior Deacon whispers in the ear of the Senior Deacon the word RABBONI. (In many Lodges, the Past Master's word, GIBLEM, is used as pass-word for this Degree, and the word RABBONI,[1] as the real word.)

S. D.—The word is right. You will wait until the Most Excellent Master is made acquainted with your request, and his answer returned.

Senior Deacon repairs to the Right Worshipful Master in the east, and gives six raps at the door.

Master—Who comes there?

S. D.—A worthy brother, who has been regularly initiated as an Entered Apprentice; passed to the Degree of a Fellow Craft; raised to the sublime Degree of a Master Mason; advanced to the honorary Degree of a Mark Master; presided as Master in the chair, and now wishes for further light in Masonry, by being received and acknowledged as a Most Excellent Master.

Master—Is it of his own free-will and accord he makes this request?

S. D.—It is.

Master—Is he duly and truly prepared?

S. D.—He is.

Master—Is he worthy and qualified?

S. D.—He is.

---

[1] "She turned herself, and saith unto him, RABBONI; which is to say Master."
—St. John, xx. 16.

Master—Has he made suitable proficiency in the preceding Degrees?

S. D.—He has.

Master—By what further right or benefit does he expect to obtain this favor?

S. D.—By the benefit of a pass-word.

Master—Has he a pass-word?

S. D.—He has not; but I have it for him.

Master—Give it.

Senior Deacon whispers in his ear the word RABBONI.

Master—The pass is right. Since he comes endowed with all these necessary qualifications, let him enter this Lodge of Most Excellent Masters, in the name of the Lord.

The door is then flung open, and the Senior Deacon receives the candidate upon the keystone. The candidate is then walked six times around the Lodge by the Senior Deacon, moving with the sun. The first time they pass around the Lodge, when opposite the Junior Warden, he gives one rap with the gavel; when opposite the Senior Warden, he does the same, and likewise when opposite the Right Worshipful Master. The second time around each gives two blows; the third, three, and so on, until they arrive to six. (See Note K, Appendix.)

During this time the Right Worshipful Master reads the following verses from Psalm CXII:

"I was glad when they said unto me, Let us go into the house of the Lord. (● ●)

"Our feet shall stand within thy gates, O Jerusalem. Jerusalem is builded as a city that is compact together. (● ● ●)

"Whither the tribes go up, the tribes of the Lord, unto the testimony of Israel, to give thanks unto the name of the Lord. (● ● ● ●)

"For there are set thrones of judgment, the thrones of the house of David. (● ● ● ● ●)

"Pray for the peace of Jerusalem: they shall prosper that love thee. Peace be within thy walls, and prosperity within thy palaces. (● ● ● ● ● ●)

"For my brethren and companions' sakes, I will now say, Peace be within thee. Because of the house of the Lord our God, I will seek thy good."

The reading of the foregoing is so timed as not to be fully ended until the Senior Deacon and candidate have performed the sixth revolution. Immediately after this the Senior Deacon and candidate arrive at the Junior Warden's station in the south, where the same questions are asked and the same answers returned as at the door. (Who comes there? &c.) The Junior Warden then directs the candidate to pass on to the Senior Warden in the west, for further examination; where the same questions are asked and answers returned as before.   The Senior Warden directs him to be conducted to the Right Worshipful Master in the east, for further examination. The Right Worshipful Master asks the same questions and receives the same answers as before.

Master (to Senior Deacon).—Please to conduct the candidate back to the west, from whence he came, and put him in the care of the Senior Warden, and request him to teach the candidate how to approach the east, by advancing upon six upright regular steps to the sixth step, and place him in a position to take upon him the solemn oath, or obligation, of a Most Excellent Master Mason.

The candidate is conducted back to the west, and the Senior Warden teaches him how to approach the east in this Degree. First, by taking the first step in Masonry, as in the Entered Apprentice's Degree, that is, stepping off with the left foot, and bringing up the right foot so as to form a square; then taking the steps as directed in the Fellow Craft Degree, and so on up to this one—beginning always with the Entered Apprentice's step. (See Fig. 14, p. 93.)

On arriving at the altar the candidate kneels on both knees, and places both hands on the Bible, square, and compasses. The Master then comes forward and addresses him:

Master—Brother, you are now placed in a proper position to take upon you the solemn oath or obligation of a Most Excellent Master Mason, which I assure you, as before, is neither to affect your religion nor politics.   If you are willing to take it, repeat your name and say after me:

I, Peter Gabe, of my own free-will and accord, in presence of Almighty God and this Lodge of Most Excellent Master Masons, erected to Him and dedicated to King Solomon, do hereby and hereon, most solemnly and sincerely promise and swear, in addition to my former obligations, that I will not give the secrets of Most Excellent Master to any one of an inferior Degree, nor to any person in the known world, except it be to a true and lawful brother of this Degree, and within the body of a just and lawfully constituted Lodge of such; and not unto him nor them whom I shall hear so to be, but unto him and them only whom I shall find so to be, after strict trial and due examination, or lawful information.

Furthermore do I promise and swear, that I will obey all regular signs and summonses handed, sent, or thrown to me from a brother of this Degree, or from the body of a just and lawfully constituted Lodge of such; provided it be within the length of my cable-tow.

Furthermore do I promise and swear, that I will support the Constitution of the General Grand Royal Arch Chapter of the United States; also, that of the Grand Chapter of this State, under which this Lodge is held, and conform to all the by-laws, rules, and regulations of this, or any other Lodge of which I may hereafter become a member.

Furthermore do I promise and swear, that I will aid and assist all poor and indigent brethren of this Degree, their widows and orphans, wheresoever dispersed around the globe, as far as in my power, without injuring myself or family.

Furthermore do I promise and swear, that the secrets of a

FIG. 28

SIGN OF A MOST EXCELLENT MASTER

brother of this Degree, given to me in charge as such, and I knowing them to be such, shall remain as secret and inviolable in my breast as in his own, murder and treason excepted, and the same left to my own free-will and choice.

Furthermore do I promise and swear, that I will not wrong this

Lodge of Most Excellent Master Masons, nor a brother of this Degree, to the value of any thing, knowingly, myself, nor suffer it to be done by others if in my power to prevent it.

Furthermore do I promise and swear, that I will dispense light and knowledge to all ignorant and uninformed brethren at all times, as far as is in my power, without material injury to myself or family. To all which I do most solemnly swear, with a fixed and steady purpose of mind in me to keep and perform the same; binding myself under no less penalty than to have my breast torn open, and my heart and vitals taken from thence, and exposed to rot on the dunghill, if ever I violate any part of this, my solemn oath, or obligation, of a Most Excellent Master Mason. So help me God, and keep me steadfast in the due performance of the same.

Master (to the candidate).—Detach your hands and kiss the book six times.[1] (Candidate obeys.) You will now rise and

FIG. 29

GRIP OF A MOST EXCELLENT MASTER

receive from me the sign, grip, and word of a Most Excellent Master Mason.

[1] We have seen in the Masonic ceremonies a constant reiteration of the number *three*, and sometimes thrice repeated, which is called giving the grand honors of Masonry. There must have been some cause or reason for this custom, now unknown. And I will venture to say, that its original intention was in honor and out of reverence to the ancient Trinity. The practice seems to be kept up by the Church of Rome, which goes to corroborate this opinion. One of the rules established by the reverend mother abbess of the Ursuline Convent at Charlestown, as reported by Miss Reed, one of the novices in that institution, is, "before entering the room, to give *three knocks* on the door, accompanied with some religious ejaculation, and wait until they are answered by *three* from within." The Mason will see that this is an exact copy of his rules and practice.

The reader has observed that the number *six*, in the Degree under consideration, is particularly respected. In the opening scene of initiations, not noticed above, the candidate is prepared with a rope wound six times round his body, and is then conducted to the door of the Lodge, against which he gives six distinct knocks, which are answered by the same number from within; and, when admitted, he is walked six times around the Lodge, *moving with the sun*. On the contrary, the brethren more advanced form a procession, as above stated, and march six times around the Lodge, *against* the course of the sun. Masons from habit pass through these ceremonies, without stopping to examine into their meaning and original intention.

The Druids also paid great veneration to the number six. "As to what remains," says Mayo (vol. II. p. 239), "respecting the superstitions of the Druids, I know not

The sign is given by placing your two hands, one on each breast, the fingers meeting in the centre of the body, and jerking them apart as though you were trying to tear open your breast. It alludes to the penalty of the obligation. (See Fig. 28.)

The grip is given by taking each other by the right hand, and clasping them so that each compress the third finger of the other with his thumb. (If one hand is large and the other small, they cannot both give the grip at the same time.) It is called the grip of all grips, because it is said to cover all the preceding grips. (See Fig. 29.)

Master (holding candidate by his hand and placing the inside of his right foot to the inside of candidate's right foot) whispers in his ear—RABBONI.

Should there be more than one candidate for initiation, the ceremony stops here until the others are advanced thus far, and then they all receive the remainder together.

A noise of shuffling feet is now heard in the Lodge, which is purposely made by some of the members.

Master (to Senior Warden).—What is the cause of all this confusion?

S. W.—Is not this the day set apart for the celebration of the cope-stone, Right Worshipful?

Master—Ah, I had forgotten. (To Secretary.) Is it so, Brother Secretary?

Sec. (looking at his book).—It is, Right Worshipful.

Master (to Senior Warden).—Brother Senior, assemble the brethren and form a procession, for the purpose of celebrating the cope-stone.

The candidate now stands aside, while the brethren assemble and form a procession, double file, and march six times around the Lodge, against the course of the sun, singing from the text-book the first three verses of the Most Excellent Master's Song:

> All hail to the morning that bids us rejoice;
> The Temple's completed, exalt high each voice;
> The cope-stone is finished, our labor is o'er;
> The sound of the gavel shall hail us no more.

---

what was the foundation of the religious respect which they had for the number six; but it is certain they preferred it to all other numbers. It was the sixth day of the moon that they performed their principal ceremonies of religion, and that they began the year. They went six in number to gather the mistletoe; and in monuments now extinct we often find six of these priests together."—*Fellow's Inquiry into the Origin, History, and Purport of Freemasonry*, p. 318.

> To the power Almighty, who ever has guided
> The tribes of old Israel, exalting their fame;
> To Him who hath governed our hearts undivided,
> Let's send forth our voices to praise His great name.

> Companions assemble on this joyful day
> (The occasion is glorious) the keystone to lay;
> Fulfilled is the promise, by the Ancient of Days,
> To bring forth the cope-stone with shouting and praise.

The keystone is now brought forward and placed in its proper place; that is, two pillars or columns, called Jachin and Boaz (see pp. 71 und 83), each about five feet high, are set up, and an arch placed on them, made of planks or boards, in imitation of block-work, in the centre of which is a mortise left for the reception of a keystone; the Most Excellent Master takes the keystone and steps up into a chair, and places it into the arch, and drives it down to its place by giving it six raps with his gavel.[1]

As soon as this ceremony is through, all the brethren move around as before, continuing the song:

> There is no more occasion
> For level or plumb-line,
> For trowel or gavel,
> For compass or square.

As they come to these words, all the brethren divest themselves of their jewels, aprons, sashes, &c., and hang them on the arch as they pass round.

> Our works are completed,
> The ark safely seated,
> And we shall be greeted
> As workmen most rare.

The Ark, which all this time has been carried round by four of the brethren, is brought forward and placed on the altar, and a pot of incense[2] is placed on the ark.

---

[1] During the ceremonies two pillars are erected, each of about five feet high, and an arch placed over them, made in imitation of block-work, in the centre of which a mortise is left for the reception of a KEYSTONE; the Most Excellent Master, taking the keystone in his hand, places it in the arch, and drives it home with six raps of his gavel.—*Historical Landmarks*, vol. II. p. 128.

[2] This pot contains gum camphor or other inflammable matter.

Now those that are worthy,
    Our toils who have shared,
And proved themselves faithful,
    Shall meet their reward;
Their virtue and knowledge,
    Industry and skill,
Have our approbation—
    Have gained our good-will.

The brethren now all halt, and face inward to the altar, and beckon the candidate to come forward and join in the ceremonies, which he does.

We accept and receive them,
    Most Excellent Masters,
Invested with honor
    And power to preside
Among worthy craftsmen,
    Wherever assembled,
The knowledge of Masons
    To spread far and wide.

As they begin the next verses, each one throws up his hands and rolls his eyes upward—giving a sign of admiration or astonishment like that described (see p. 203) as having been expressed by the Queen of Sheba on first viewing Solomon's Temple—and keeps them in that position while singing these two verses of the song: (See Fig. 30.)

Almighty Jehovah,
    Descend now, and fill
This Lodge with thy glory,
    Our hearts with good-will;
Preside at our meetings,
    Assist us to find
True pleasure in teaching
    Good-will to mankind.

Thy wisdom inspired
The great institution;
Thy strength shall support,
    Till Nature expire;
And when the creation
Shall fall into ruin,
Its beauty shall rise
    Through the midst of the fire.

The brothers now all join hands as in opening, and while in this attitude the Right Worshipful Master reads the following passage of Scripture, 2 Chron. VII. 1, 4.

FIG. 30

SIGN OF ADMIRATION, OR ASTONISHMENT

"Now when Solomon had made an end of praying, the fire came down from heaven, and consumed the burnt-offering and the sacrifices; and the glory of the Lord filled the house. And the priests could not enter into the house of the Lord, because the glory of the Lord had filled the Lord's house. And when all the children of Israel saw how the fire came down, and the glory of the Lord upon the house, they bowed themselves with their faces to the ground upon the pavement, and worshipped and praised the Lord, saying, For he is good (here the Master, who is high-priest of the Chapter, kneels and joins hands with the rest), for his mercy endureth forever."

They all then repeat in concert the words, "*For he is good* (here one of the brethren, standing behind the candidate, throws a piece of blazing gum-camphor or other combustible matter into the *pot of incense* standing on the altar, around which the brethren are kneeling), *for his mercy endureth forever,*" six times, each time bowing their heads low toward the floor. The members now balance six times, as in opening (see page 203), rise and balance six times more, then, disengaging themselves from each other, take their seats.

Master (to candidate.)—Brother, your admission to this Degree of Masonry is a proof of the good opinion the brethren of this Lodge entertain of your Masonic abilities. Let this consideration induce you to be careful of forfeiting, by misconduct and inattention to our rules, that esteem which has raised you to the rank you now possess. It is one of your great duties, as a Most Excellent Master, to dispense light and truth to the uninformed Mason; and I need not remind you of the impossibility of complying with this obligation without possessing an accurate acquaintance with the lectures of each degree. If you are not already completely conversant in all the Degrees heretofore conferred on you remember that an indulgence, prompted by a belief that you will apply yourself with double diligence to make yourself so, has induced the brethren to accept you. Let it, therefore, be your unremitting study to acquire such a degree of knowledge and information as shall enable you to discharge with propriety the various duties incumbent on you, and to preserve unsullied the title now conferred upon you of a Most Excellent Master.

This charge closes the initiation, and a motion is generally made to adjourn, and close the Lodge.

Master (to J. W.)—Brother Junior, you will please assemble the brethren around the altar, for the purpose of closing this Lodge of Most Excellent Masters.

The brethren immediately assemble around the altar in a circle, and kneel on the right knee, put their left arms over, and join hands as before. While kneeling in this position, the Master reads the following verses from the one hundred and thirty-fourth Psalm:

"Behold, bless ye the Lord, all ye servants of the Lord, which by night stand in the house of the Lord.

"Lift up your hands in the sanctuary, and bless the Lord.

"The Lord, that made heaven and earth, bless thee out of Zion."

The Master then closes the circle as in opening, when they balance six times, rise and balance six times more, disengaging their hands, and giving the signs from this Degree downward. The Lodge is then closed as in the preceding Degrees. The following is read at closing:—

"The Lord is my shepherd; I shall not want. He maketh me to lie down in green pastures; he leadeth me beside the still waters. He restoreth my soul; he leadeth me in the paths of righteousness for his name's sake. Yea, though I walk through the valley of the shadow of death, I will fear no evil; for thou art with me; thy rod and thy staff they comfort me. Thou preparest a table before me in the presence of mine enemies; thou anointest my head with oil; my cup runneth over. Surely goodness and mercy shall follow me all the days of my life; and I will dwell in the house of the Lord forever."—*Psalm* XXIII.[1]

LECTURE ON THE SIXTH, OR MOST EXCELLENT MASTER'S DEGREE

Question. Are you a Most Excellent Master?

Answer. I am. Try me.

Q. How will you be tried?

A. By the cap stone.

Q. Why by the cap stone?

A. Because it completed King Solomon's Temple, upon the ceremonies of the dedication of which this Degree is founded.

Q. Where were you received and acknowledged as a Most Excellent Master?

A. In a regular and duly constituted Lodge of Most Excellent Masters.

Q. How gained you admission?

A. By six distinct knocks. (● ● ● ● ● ●)

Q. To what do the six distinct knocks allude?

A. To the Sixth Degree of Masonry, it being that upon which I was about to enter.

Q. What was said to you from within?

A. Who comes here?

Q. Your answer?

A. A worthy brother who has been duly initiated, passed to the degree of Fellow Craft, raised to the sublime degree of Master Mason, advanced to the degree of Mark Master, and regularly passed the chair, now wishes for further promotion in Masonry, by being received and acknowledged as a Most Excellent Master.

Q. What were you then asked?

A. If it was an act of my own free will and accord; if I was worthy and well qualified; if I had made suitable proficiency in the preceding degree, and was properly vouched for, all of which

---

[1] "Recent discoveries in Ethiopia have brought to light," says a writer on the Egyptian antiquities in the British Museum, "arches regularly constructed with the *keystone*. The same arch is also found in the vaulted roof of a small building or portico in the Egyptian style, which is attached to one of the sides of the largest pyramids at Assour. At Jebel Barkal, Mr. Waddington observed an arched roof in a portico attached to a pyramid." These pyramids are supposed to be of higher antiquity than the building of King Solomon's Temple.—*Theo. Phil.*, p. 208.

being answered in the affirmative, I was asked by what right or benefit I expected to gain this important privilege.

Q. Your answer?

A. By the benefit of the pass.

Q. Give it. (Word—Mark Well.)

Q. What was then said to you?

A. I was directed to wait until the Right Worshipful Master could be informed of my request, and his answer returned.

Q. What was his answer?

A. Let the candidate enter.

Q. How were you then disposed of?

A. I was conducted *six* times round the Lodge, to the Worshipful Senior Warden in the West, where the same questions were asked and answers returned as at the door.

Q. How did the Worshipful Senior Warden dispose of you?

A. He directed me to be conducted to the Right Worshipful Master in the East, where the same questions were asked and answers returned as before.

Q. How did the Right Worshipful Master dispose of you?

A. He ordered me to be conducted to the Worshipful Senior Warden in the West, who taught me to approach to the altar, advancing by six upright Masonic steps, my feet forming a square and my body erect, to the Right Worshipful Master.

Q. What did the Right Worshipful Master do with you?

A. He made me a Most Excellent Master.

Q. How?

A. In due form.

Q. What is that due form?

A. Kneeling upon both knees, both hands covering the Holy Bible, square and compasses, my body erect, in which due form I took upon myself the solemn oath of a Most Excellent Master.

Q. Have you that obligation?

A. I have.

Q. Will you give it?

A. I will with your assistance.

Q. Proceed. (I, A. B., etc., etc. See obligation.)

Q. Have you a sign belonging to this degree?

A. I have several.

Q. Show me a sign. (Give sign.)

Q. What is that called?

A. A duegard.

Q. Show me another sign. (Gives sign.)

Q. What is that called?

A The sign.

Q. To what does it allude?

A. To the penalty of my obligation, that I would have my breast torn open—my heart torn out and exposed to rot upon the dung hill, sooner than divulge any of the secrets of this degree unlawfully.

Q. Show me another sign. (Give sign of admiration.)

Q. What is that called?

A. The sign of admiration.

Q. To what does it allude?

A. To the wonder and admiration of our ancient brethren who were present and permitted to view the interior of that magnificent edifice which King Solomon had erected, and was about to dedicate to the service of the Supreme Being.

Q. Have you a grip?

A. I have.

Q. Communicate it to a brother? (Give grip.)

Q. Has it a name?

A. It has.

Q. Give it. (Rabboni.)

Q. What does it signify?

A. Good Master or Most Excellent Master.

Q. What is it otherwise called?

A. The cover grip.

Q. Why?

A. Because as this covers grips of preceding degrees, so should we as Most Excellent Masters, considering that man in his best estate is subject to frailties and errors, endeavor to cover his faults and imperfections with the broad mantle of charity and brotherly love.

Q. When originated this grip?

A. At the completion of the temple. When King Solomon entered he was so well pleased with the master builder that he took him by the right hand and exclaimed, Hail, Rabboni, which signifies Good Master and Most Excellent Master.

Q. What followed?

A. A procession was formed, the ark safely seated, the cap stone placed in the principal arch, and Lodge closed with solemn invocations to Deity.

KEYSTONE

ROYAL ARCH, OR SEVENTH DEGREE

THE Royal Arch Degree seems not to have been known to what are called *modern* Masons as late as about 1750. That portion of the old Freemasons who met at the famous Apple-Tree Tavern, in 1717, and formed the society upon somewhat new principles, that is, so far as to admit into fellowship, indiscriminately, respectable individuals of all professions, were denominated, by the non-adherents to this plan, *modern* Masons. This affair caused the division of the Masonic Society into two parties, which continued till 1813, nearly one hundred years. To the rivalry occasioned by this schism, Masonry, it is presumed, is mainly indebted for the great celebrity it has obtained in the world.

It appears that the non-conformists to this new scheme, who considered themselves the orthodox party, by rummaging among the old records of the Order, first discovered the Royal Arch Degree, which had probably lain dormant for centuries; during which time, it would appear, the society had been confined almost exclusively to operative masons; who continued the ceremonies only of the apprentice, fellow-craft or journeyman, and master mason, these being deemed appropriate to their occupation.

A society of Royal Arch Masons is called a Chapter, and not a Lodge, as in the previous Degrees. All Chapters of Royal Arch Masons are "dedicated to Zerubbabel," and the symbolic color of this Degree is scarlet. The several Degrees of Mark Master, Present or Past Master, and Most Excellent Master, are given only under the sanction of the Royal Arch Chapter; and a Master Mason who applies for these Degrees usually enters the Chapter also, and sometimes the four degrees are given at once. If he takes the four, he is only balloted for once, viz.: in the Mark Master's Degree. Candidates receiving this Degree are said to be "exalted to the most sublime Degree of the Royal Arch."

It is a point of the Royal Arch Degree not to assist, or be present, at the conferring of this Degree upon more or less than three candidates at one time. If there are not three candidates present, one or two companions, as the case may be, volunteer to represent candidates, so as to make the requisite number, or a "team," as it is technically styled, and accompany the candidate or candidates through all the stages of exaltation.

At the destruction of Jerusalem by Nebuchadnezzar, three Most Excellent Masters were carried captives to Babylon, where they remained seventy years, and were liberated by Cyrus, King of Persia. They returned to Jerusalem to assist in rebuilding the Temple, after travelling over rugged roads on foot. They arrived at the outer veil of the Tabernacle, which was erected near the ruins of the Temple. This Tabernacle was an oblong square, enclosed by four veils, or curtains, and divided into separate apartments by four cross veils, including the west end veil or entrance. The veils were parted in the centre, and guarded by four guards, with drawn swords.

At the east end of the Tabernacle, Haggai, Joshua, and Zerubbabel usually sat in grand council, to examine all who wished to be employed in the noble and glorious work of rebuilding the Temple. Since that time, every Chapter of Royal Arch Masons, if properly formed, represents the Tabernacle erected by our ancient brethren, near the ruins of King Solomon's Temple, and our engraving shows the interior arrangement of a Chapter of the Royal Arch Degree.[1] (See Fig. 31.)

These three Most Excellent Masters, on their arrival, were introduced to the Grand Council, and employed, furnished with tools, and directed to commence their labors at the northeast corner of the ruins of the old Temple, and to clear away and remove the rubbish, in order to lay the foundation of the new. The Grand Council also gave them strict orders to preserve whatever should fall in their way (such as specimens of ancient architecture, &c.,) and bring it up for their inspection.

Among the discoveries made by the three Masters was a secret vault in which they found treasures of great benefit to the craft, &c. The ceremony of exalting companions to this Degree, is a recapitulation of the adventures of these three Most Excellent Masters, and hence it is that three candidates are necessary for an initiation.

---

[1] In America, we find an essential variation from any other system of the Royal Arch. The names of the officers vary materially, as also do the ceremonies. As in Ireland, it constitutes the Seventh Degree, although the intermediate steps are different. In Ireland they are: 1. E. A. P.; 2. F. C.; 3. M. M.; 4. P. M.; 5. Excellent; 6. Super-Excellent; 7. Royal Arch: while in America the Fourth is Mark Master; 5. P. M.; 6. Most Excellent Master; 7. Royal Arch.—*Origin of the English Royal Arch*, p. 58.

The Grand Council consists of the Most Excellent High Priest, King, and Holy Scribe. The High Priest is dressed in a white robe, with a breastplate of cut glass, consisting of twelve pieces, an apron, and a mitre. The king wears a scarlet robe, apron, and crown. The mitre and crown are generally made of pasteboard; sometimes they are made of most splendid materials, gold and silver velvet; but these are kept for public occasions. The mitre has the words, "Holiness to the Lord," in gold letters, across the forehead. The scribe wears a purple robe, apron, and turban.

A Chapter of Royal Arch Masons consists of nine officers, as follows:

1. High Priest, or Master. (Joshua.)
2. King, or Senior Grand Warden. (Zerubbabel.)
3. Scribe, or Junior Grand Warden. (Haggai.)
4. Captain of the Host (as Marshal, or Master of Ceremonies), or Senior Deacon.
5. Principal Sojourner, who represents the Junior Deacon.
6. Royal Arch Captain, who represents the Master Overseer.
7. Grand Master of the Third Veil, or Senior Overseer.
8. Grand Master of the Second Veil, or Junior Overseer.
9. Grand Master of the First Veil.

In addition to these, three other officers are usually present, viz., Secretary, a Treasurer, and a Tyler, or sentinel.

The officers and companions of the Chapter being stationed as in the engraving (see Fig. 31), the High Priest proceeds to business as follows:

High Priest—Companions,[1] I am about to open a Chapter of Royal Arch Masons in this place, for the dispatch of business, and will thank you for your attention and assistance. If there is any person present who is not a companion Royal Arch Mason, he is requested to retire from the room.

After waiting for any stranger or brother not of this degree to retire, he gives one rap with the gavel, which brings up the Captain of the Host.

High Priest—Companion Captain, the first care of congregated Masons?

[1] The members of this Degree are denominated *companions*, and are "entitled to a full explanation of the *mysteries* of the Order"; whereas in the former Degrees they are recognized by the common, familiar appellation of brothers, and kept in a state of profound ignorance of the *sublime secret* which is disclosed in this Chapter. This accords with the custom of Pythagoras, who thus distinguished his pupils. After a probation of five years, as before stated, they were admitted into the presence of the preceptor, called his *companions*, and permitted freely to converse with him. Previously to the expiration of that term he delivered his instructions to them from behind a screen.—*Fellows's Inquiry into the Origin, History, and Purport of Freemasonry*, p. 321.

FIG. 81

ROYAL ARCH CHAPTER

1. Treasurer. 2. Secretary. 3. King. 4. High Priest. 5. Scribe. 6. Captain of the Host. 7. Principal Sojourner. 8. Royal Arch Captain. 9. Grand Master of the Third Veil. 10. Grand Master of the Second Veil. 11. Grand Master of the First Veil. 12. Burning Bush. 13. Altar.

Captain (placing the palm of his right hand to his forehead, as if to shade his eyes).—To see the Tabernacle duly guarded, Most Excellent. (For this sign, see Fig. 36.)

High Priest—Attend to that part of your duty, and inform the Guard that we are about to open a Chapter of Royal Arch Masons in this place for the dispatch of business; direct him to guard accordingly.

The Captain of the Host stations the Guard at the outside of the door, gives him his orders, closes the door, and makes an alarm of three times three (●●● ●●● ●●●) on the inside, to ascertain that the Guard is on his post: the Guard answers by nine corresponding raps. The Captain of the Host then gives one, and Guard does the same. The Captain then returns to his post.

Captain (to High Priest).—The Chapter is duly guarded, Most Excellent.

High Priest—How guarded?

Captain—By a companion of this Degree at the outer avenue, with a drawn sword in his hand.

High Priest—His duty there?

Captain—To observe the approach of all cowans and eaves-droppers, and see that none pass or repass but such as are duly qualified.

High Priest—Companions, we will be clothed.

The companions place the furniture of the Chapter in proper order, clothe with their various jewels, robes, and badges of this Degree, and draw aside the veils, which brings the hall into one apartment, and resume their seats. The High Priest then gives two raps with the gavel, which brings all the officers on their feet, while the following lecture is given, or questions asked, by the High Priest, and answered by the Captain of the Host.

High Priest—Companion Captain of the Host, are you a Royal Arch Mason?

Captain—I am, that I am.

High Priest—How shall I know you to be a Royal Arch Mason?

Captain—By three times three.

High Priest—Where were you made a Royal Arch Mason?

Captain—In a just and legally constituted Chapter of Royal Arch Masons, consisting of Most Excellent High Priest, King and Scribe, Captain of the Host, Principal Sojourner, Royal Arch Captain, and the three Grand Masters of the veils, assembled in a room or place representing the Tabernacle erected by our ancient brethren near the ruins of King Solomon's Temple.

High Priest—Where is the High Priest stationed, and what are his duties?

Captain—He is stationed in the sanctum sanctorum. His duty, with the King and Scribe, is to sit in the Grand Council, to form plans, and give directions to the workmen.

High Priest—The King's station and duty?

Captain—Station, at the right hand of the High Priest; duty, to aid him by his advice and counsel, and in his absence to preside.

High Priest—The Scribe's station and duty?

Captain—Station, at the left hand of the High Priest; duty, to assist him and the King in the discharge of their duties, and to preside in their absence.

High Priest—The Captain of the Host's station and duty?

Captain—Station, at the right hand in front of Grand Council; duty, to receive orders, and see them duly executed.

High Priest—The Principal Sojourner's station and duty?

Captain—Station, at the left hand in front of Grand Council; duty, to bring the blind by a way that they know not; to lead them in paths they have not known; to make darkness light before them, and crooked things straight.

High Priest—The Royal Arch Captain's station and duty?

Captain—Station, at the inner veil, or entrance to the sanctum sanctorum; duty, to guard the same, and see that none pass but such as are duly qualified, and have the proper pass-words, and the signet of truth.

High Priest—What is the color of his banner?

Captain—White, and is emblematical of that purity of heart and rectitude of conduct which are essential to obtain admission into the divine sanctum sanctorum above.

High Priest—The stations and duties of the three Grand Masters of the veils?

Captain—Station, at the entrance of their respective veils; duty, to guard the same, and see that none pass but such as are duly qualified, and in possession of the proper pass-words and tokens.

High Priest—What are the colors of their banners?

Captain—That of the third, scarlet; which is emblematical of fervency and zeal, and the appropriate color of the Royal Arch Degree. It admonishes us to be fervent in the exercise of our devotions to God, and zealous in our endeavors to promote the happiness of men. Of the second, purple; which being produced by a due mixture of blue and scarlet, the former of which is the characteristic color of the symbolic, or three first Degrees, it teaches us to cultivate and improve that spirit of harmony between the brethren of the symbolic Degrees and the companions of the sublime Degrees, which should ever distinguish the members of a society founded upon the principles of everlasting truth and universal philanthropy. Of the first, blue; the peculiar color of the three ancient, or symbolical Degrees. It is an emblem of universal friendship and benevolence, and instructs us that in the mind of a Mason those virtues should be as expansive as the blue arch of heaven itself.

High Priest—The Treasurer's station and duty?

Captain—Station, at the right hand in rear of the Captain of the Host; his duty, to keep a just and regular account of all the property and funds of the Chapter placed in his hands, and exhibit them to the Chapter when called upon for that purpose.

High Priest—The Secretary's place in the Chapter?

Captain—Station, at the left in rear of the Principal Sojourner; his duty, to issue the orders and notifications of his superior officers, record the proceedings of the Chapter proper to be written, to receive all moneys due the Chapter, and pay them over to the Treasurer.

High Priest—Guard's place and duty?

Captain—His station is at the outer avenue of the Chapter; his duty, to guard against the approach of cowans and eavesdroppers, and suffer none to pass or repass, but such as are duly qualified.

High Priest (addressing the Chapter).—Companions, you will assemble round the altar, for the purpose of assisting me in opening a Chapter of Royal Arch Masons.

All the members present (except the Grand Council) approach the altar, and, forming a circle, kneel, each upon his right knee. An opening in the circle is left for the High Priest, the King, and the Scribe. The High Priest rises and reads from the Second Epistle of Paul to the Thessalonians, chap. III., vs. 6 to 18:—

"Now we command you, brethren, in the name of our Lord Jesus Christ, that ye withdraw yourselves from every brother that walketh disorderly, and not after the tradition which ye have received of us. For yourselves know how ye ought to follow us; for we behaved not ourselves disorderly among you; neither did we eat any man's bread for naught; but wrought with labor and travail night and day, that we might not be chargeable to any of you; not because we have not power, but to make ourselves an example unto you to follow us." &c.

After the reading, the High Priest, the King, and the Scribe approach the altar and take their places in the circle, kneeling with the rest, the King on the right, and the Scribe on the left of the High Priest. Each one now crosses his arms and gives his right hand to his left-hand companion, and his left hand to his right-hand companion. This constitutes the living arch under which the Grand Omnific Royal Arch Word must be given, but it must also be given by three times three, as hereafter explained.

The High Priest now whispers in the King's ear the pass-word RABBONI.

The King whispers it to the companion on his right, and he to the next one, and so on until it comes round to the Scribe, who whispers it to the High Priest.

High Priest—The word is right.

The companions now all balance three times three with their arms; that is, they raise their arms and let them fall upon their knees three times in concert—after a short pause, three times more, and after another pause, three times more. They then rise and give all the signs, from the Entered Apprentice up to this Degree, after which they join in squads of three for giving the Grand Omnific Royal Arch Word, as follows:

Each one takes hold with his right hand of the right wrist of his companion on the left, and with his left hand takes hold of the left wrist of his companion on the right. Each one then places his right foot forward with the hollow in front, so that the toe touches the heel of his companion on the right. This is called "three times three;" that is, three right feet forming a triangle, three left hands forming a triangle, and three right hands forming a triangle. In this position each repeats the following:

> As we three did agree,
> In peace, love, and unity,
> The Sacred Word to keep,
> So we three do agree,
> In peace, love, and unity,
> The Sacred Word to search;
> Until we three,
> Or three such as we, shall agree
> To close this Royal Arch.

They then balance three times three, bringing the right hand with some violence down upon the left. The right hands are then raised above their heads, and the words, Jah-buh-lun, Je-ho-vah, G-o-d,[1] are given at low breath, each companion pronouncing the syllables or letters alternately, as follows:

---

[1] Cole adopts the following sentiment of a brother Mason: "In the R. A. (Royal Arch) Mason's Degree I beheld myself exalted to the top of *Pisgah*, an extensive scene opened to my view of the glory and goodness of the M. E. H. P. (Most Excellent High Priest) of our salvation. I dug deep for *hidden treasures*, found them, and *regained* the *omnific word*."

"If we pass on to the Royal Arch," says the Rev. G. Oliver, in his Lectures on

Fig. 32

THREE TIMES THREE

1st.	2nd.	3d.
Jah	buh	lun.
. . . .	Jah	buh
lun		
. . . . Jah		
buh	lun.	
Je	ho	vah.

Freemasonry, "we receive a wonderful accession of knowledge, and find every thing *made perfect*; for this is the *ne plus ultra* of Masonry, and can never be exceeded by any human institution."—*Fellows's Inquiry into the Origin, History, and Purport of Freemasonry*, p. 322.

A Degree indescribably more august, sublime, and important than any which precede it, and is, in fact, the summit and perfection of ancient Masonry. It impresses on our minds a belief in the being of a God, without beginning of days or end of years, the great and incomprehensible Alpha and Omega, and reminds us of the reverence which is due to His Holy Name.—*Historical Landmarks*, vol. I. p. 86.

. . . . Je . . . . ho
vah. . . . .
. . . . Je
ho . . . . vah.
G . . . . o . . . . d.
. . . . G . . . . o
d. . . . .
. . . . G
o . . . . d.¹

After the word is thus given, the High Priest inquires if the word is right.

Each squad replies that it is right.

The officers and companions resume their seats. The High Priest raps three times with his gavel, the King repeats it, as also the Scribes; this is done three times (●●● ●●● ●●●).

High Priest (rising).—I now declare this Chapter of Royal Arch Masons opened in due and ancient form; and I hereby forbid all improper conduct whereby the peace and harmony of this Chapter may be disturbed, under no less penalties than the by-laws, or a majority of the Chapter, may see fit to inflict.

High Priest (to Captain of the Host).—Companion Captain, please to inform the Guard that the Chapter is open.

The Captain proceeds on this duty, while the Secretary reads the minutes of the last meeting. Should there be any candidates to be balloted for, this is the first business in order. If one or more candidates are waiting without, the Principal Sojourner goes to the preparation-room to get them ready. If there are not three of them, a companion or companions volunteer to make the trio, as not less than three can perform the ceremonies. The three take off their coats, when the Principal Sojourner ties bandages over their eyes, and, taking a long rope, coils it seven times round the body of each, leaving about three feet slack between.

¹ This ineffable name (in INDIA) was *Aum*, which, in its triliteral form, was significant of the creative, preservative, and destroying power, that is, of Brahma, Vishnu, and Siva.—*Lexicon*, p. 146.

JEHOVAH. Of the varieties of this sacred name in use among the different nations of the earth, three particularly merit the attention of Royal Arch Masons:

1. JAH. This name of God is found in the 68th Psalm, v. 4.

2. BAAL OR BEL. This word signifies a *lord, master, or possessor*, and hence it was applied by many of the nations of the East to denote the Lord of all things, and the Master of the world.

3. ON. This was the name by which JEHOVAH was worshipped among the Egyptians.

I have made these remarks on the three names of God in Chaldaic, Syriac and Egyptian, *Baal, Jah*, and *On*, in the expectation that my Royal Arch Companions will readily recognize them in a corrupted form.—*Lexicon*.

Principal Sojourner—Three worthy brothers, who have been initiated, passed, and raised to the sublime Degree of Master Masons, advanced to the honorary Degree of Mark Master, presided as Master in the chair, and, at the completion and dedication of the Temple, were received and acknowledged Most Excellent Masters; and now wish for further light in Masonry, by being exalted to the august sublime Degree of the Holy Royal Arch.
- Captain (to candidates).—Is it of your own free-will and accord you make this request?

First Candidate (prompted).—It is,

Captain (to Principal Sojourner).—Are they duly andtruly prepared?

Principal Sojourner—They are.

Captain—Have they made suitable proficiency in thepreceding Degrees?

Principal Sojourner—They have.

Captain—By what further right or benefit do they expect to gain admission to this Chapter of Royal Arch Masons?

Principal Sojourner—By the benefit of a pass.

Captain—Have they that pass?

Principal Sojourner—They have it not; but I have it for them.

The Captain of the Host goes to the door, opens it, and says:

Captain—It is our Most Excellent High Priest's order, that the candidates enter this Chapter of Royal Arch Masons, and be received under a Living Arch.

Principal Sojourner (leading the candidates by the rope).—Companions, you will follow me. (Leads them in.) I will bring the blind by a way they know not: I will lead them in paths they have not known; I will make darkness light before them, and crooked things straight. These things will I do unto them, and will not forsake them. Stoop low, brethren: he that humbleth himself shall be exalted.

Meantime the brethren, or companions of the Chapter, form two lines facing each other, from the door to the centre of the room, and each one takes hold and locks his fingers with those of his opposite companion. As the candidates pass under this Living Arch, each couple place their knuckles upon the necks and backs of the candidates, kneading them pretty hard sometimes, and prostrating them on the floor. Thus they have a good deal of difficulty in forcing their way through. When they do get through, they are first conducted round the Chapter, and then to the altar, where they must kneel to receive the obligation.

Principal Sojourner (to the candidates).—Brethren, as you advance in Masonry, your obligation becomes more binding. You are now kneeling at the altar for the seventh time; and about to take a solemn oath, or obligation, which, like your former obligations, is not to interfere with the duty you owe to your country, or Maker. If you are willing to proceed, you will repeat your Christian and surname, and say after me:

I, Peter Gabe, of my own free-will and accord, in presence of Almighty God, and this Chapter of Royal Arch Masons, erected to God, and dedicated to Zerubbabel, do hereby and hereon most solemnly and sincerely promise and swear, in addition to my former obligations, that I will not reveal the secrets of this Degree to any of an inferior Degree, nor to any being in the known world, except it be to a true and lawful Companion Royal Arch Mason, or within the body of a just and legally constituted Chapter of such and never unto him, or them, whom I shall hear so to be, but to him and them only whom I shall find so to be, after strict trial and due examination, or lawful information given.

I furthermore promise and swear, that I will not wrong this Chapter of Royal Arch Masons, or a companion of this Degree, out of the value of any thing, myself, nor suffer it to be done by others, if in my power to prevent it.

I furthermore promise and swear, that I will not reveal the key to the ineffable characters of this Degree, nor retain it in my possession, but will destroy it whenever it comes to my sight.

I furthermore promise and swear, that I will not speak the Grand Omnific Royal Arch Word, which I shall hereafter receive, in any manner, except in that in which I shall receive it, which will be in the presence of three Companions Royal Arch Masons, myself making one of the number; and then by three times three, under a Living Arch, and at low breath.

I furthermore promise and swear, that I will not be at the exaltation of candidates in a clandestine Chapter, nor converse upon the secrets of this Degree with a clandestine-made Mason, or with one who has been expelled or suspended, while under that sentence.

I furthermore promise and swear, that I will not assist or be present at the exaltation of a candidate to this Degree, who has not received the Degrees of Entered Apprentice, Fellow Craft, Master Mason, Mark Master, Past Master, and Most Excellent Master.

I furthermore promise and swear, that I will not be at the exaltation of more nor less than three candidates at one and the same time.

I furthermore promise and swear, that I will not be at the forming or opening of a Chapter of Royal Arch Masons unless there be present nine Royal Arch Masons, myself making one of that number.

I furthermore promise and swear, that I will not speak evil of a Companion Royal Arch Mason, behind his back nor before his face, but will apprise him of all approaching danger, if in my power.

I furthermore promise and swear, that I will support the Constitution of the General Grand Royal Arch Chapter of the United States of America; together with that of the Grand Chapter of this State, under which this Chapter is holden; that I will stand to and abide by all the by-laws, rules, and regulations of this Chapter, or of any other Chapter of which I may hereafter become a member.

I furthermore promise and swear, that I will answer and obey all due signs and summonses handed, sent, or thrown to me from a Chapter of Royal Arch Masons, or from a Companion Royal Arch Mason, if within the length of my cable-tow.

I furthermore promise and swear, that I will not strike a Companion Royal Arch Mason, so as to draw his blood, in anger.

I furthermore promise and swear, that I will employ a Companion Royal Arch Mason in preference to any other person of equal qualifications.

I furthermore promise and swear, that I will assist a Companion Royal Arch Mason when I see him engaged in any difficulty, and will espouse his cause so far as to extricate him from the same, whether he be right or wrong.

I furthermore promise and swear, that I will keep all the secrets of a Companion Royal Arch Mason (when communicated to me as such, or I knowing them to be such), without exceptions.

I furthermore promise and swear, that I will be aiding and assisting all poor and indigent Companions Royal Arch Masons, their widows and orphans, wheresoever dispersed around the globe; they making application to me as such, and I finding them worthy, and can do it without any material injury to myself or family.

To all which I do most solemnly and sincerely promise and swear, with a firm and steadfast resolution to keep and perform the same, without any equivocation, mental reservation, or self-evasion of mind in me whatever; binding myself under no less penalty, than to have my skull smote off, and my brains exposed to the scorching rays of the meridian sun, should I knowingly or wilfully violate or transgress any part of this my solemn oath or obligation of a Royal Arch Mason. So help me God, and keep me steadfast in the due performance of the same.

Principal Sojourner—Kiss the book seven times.

The candidate kisses the book as directed.

Principal Sojourner—Companions, you will arise and follow me. For although you are obligated Royal Arch Masons, yet, as the secrets of this Degree are of infinitely more importance than any that precede it, it is necessary that you should travel through rough and rugged ways, and pass through many trials, in testimony of your fidelity to the Order, before you can be instructed in the more important secrets of this Degree.

The candidates are conducted once around the Chapter, and then again directed to kneel, while the Principal Sojourner reads the following prayer:

Supreme and inscrutable Architect of universal Nature, who, by thine Almighty word didst speak into being the stupendous arch of heaven, and, for the instruction and pleasure of thy rational creatures, didst adorn us with greater and lesser lights, thereby magnifying thy power, and endearing thy goodness unto the sons of men, we humbly adore and worship thine unspeakable perfection. We bless thee, that, when man had fallen from his innocence and his happiness, thou didst leave him the powers of reasoning, and capacity of improvement and pleasure. We thank thee, that, amid the pains and calamities of our present state, so many means of refreshment and satisfaction are reserved to us, while travelling the rugged path of life; especially would we, at this time, render thee our thanksgiving and praise for the institution, as members of which we are at this time assembled, and for all the pleasures we have derived from it. We thank thee, that the few here assembled before thee have been favored with new inducements, and been laid under new and stronger obligations of virtue and holiness. May these obligations, O blessed Father! have their full effect upon us. Teach us, we pray thee, the true reverence of thy great, mighty, and terrible Name. Inspire us with a firm and unshaken resolution in our virtuous pursuits. Give us grace diligently to search thy word in the book of nature, wherein the duties of our high vocation are inculcated with Divine authority. May the solemnity of the ceremonies of our institution be duly impressed on our minds, and have a happy and lasting effect on our lives! O Thou, who didst aforetime appear unto thy servant Moses in a flame of fire out of the midst of a bush, enkindle, we beseech thee, in each of our hearts, a flame of devotion to thee, of love to each other, and of charity to all mankind! May all thy miracles and mighty works fill us with thy dread, and thy goodness impress us with a love of thy holy name! May holiness to the Lord be engraven upon all our thoughts, words, and actions! May the incense of piety ascend continually unto thee from the altar of our hearts, and burn day and night, as a sacrifice of a sweet-smelling savor, well-pleasing unto thee! And since sin has destroyed within us the first temple of purity and innocence, may thy heavenly grace guide and assist us in rebuilding a second temple of reformation, and may the glory of this latter house be greater than the glory of the former! Amen, so mote it be.

Principal Sojourner—Companions, arise and follow me.

He now conducts them once around the Chapter, during which time he reads from the text-book the first six verses of the third chapter of Exodus:—

"Now Moses kept the flock of Jethro his father-in-law, the priest of Midian; and he led the flock to the back side of the desert, and came to the mountain of God, even to Horeb. And the angel of the Lord appeared unto him in a flame of fire out of the midst of a bush; and he looked, and behold, the bush burned with fire, and the bush was not consumed." &c.

The reading of these verses is so timed, that just when they are finished the candidates have arrived in front of a representation of the burning bush, placed in a corner of the Chapter; when the Principal Sojourner directs them to halt, and slips up the bandages from their eyes.

One of the members now personates the Deity, behind the bush, and calls out, Moses! Moses!

Principal Sojourner (answering for candidates).—Here I am.

Companion behind the bush—Draw not nigh hither: put off thy shoes from off thy feet, for the place whereon thou standest is holy ground. I am the God of thy fathers, the God of Abraham, the God of Isaac, and the God of Jacob.

Principal Sojourner directs the candidates to kneel, and he covers their faces again, and then says—And Moses hid his face, for he was afraid to look upon God.

Principal Sojourner (to candidates).—Arise, and follow me.

He then leads them three times around the Chapter, during which time he reads from the text-book 2 Chronicles, ch. XXXVI., vs. 11 to 20

"Zedekiah was one-and-twenty years old when he began to reign, and he reigned eleven years in Jerusalem. And he did that which was evil in the sight of the Lord his God, and humbled not himself before Jeremiah the prophet, speaking from the mouth of the Lord. And he also rebelled against King Nebuchadnezzar, and stiffened his neck, and hardened his heart from turning unto the Lord God of Israel. Moreover, all the chief of the priests and the people transgressed very much, after all the abominations of the heathen, and polluted the house of the Lord, which he had hallowed in Jerusalem. And the Lord God of their fathers sent to them by his messengers, because he had compassion on his people, and on his dwelling-place. But they mocked the messengers of God, and despised his Word, and misused his prophets, until the wrath of the Lord arose against his people, till there was no remedy. Therefore he brought upon them the King of the Chaldees, who slew their young men with the sword, in the house of their sanctuary, and had no compassion upon young men or maidens, old men, or him that stooped for age; he gave them all into his hand. And all the vessels of the house of God, great and small, and the treasures of the house of the Lord, and the treasures of the king, and his princes; all these he brought to Babylon. And they burnt the house of God, and brake down the wall of Jerusalem, and burnt all the palaces thereof with fire, and destroyed all the goodly vessels thereof. And them that had escaped from the sword carried he away to Babylon; where they were servants to him and his sons, until the reign of the kingdom of Persia."

When the Principal Sojourner arrives at that part of the above reading which alludes to the Chaldees killing the young men with the sword, the companions of the Chapter begin to make all sorts of queer and unearthly noises, such as rolling cannon-balls on the floor, clashing old swords, shouting, groaning, whistling, stamping, throwing down benches, &c. This noise continues during the remainder of the reading, the object being to represent the siege and destruction of Jerusalem. During this confusion the three candidates are seized, thrown upon the floor, bound hand and foot, and carried bodily into the preparation-room, when the door is closed.

In a few minutes the companions begin to shout: "Hurra for the captives!" repeating it several times.

Captain of the Host goes and opens the door, and says—Come forth! you are at liberty to return! for Cyrus has issued his proclamation to build a second Temple at Jerusalem.

Principal Sojourner (who is with the candidates).—Will you read the proclamation?

Captain of the Host reads the first three verses of the first chapter of Ezra, as follows:

"Now in the first year of Cyrus, King of Persia, the Lord stirred up the spirit of Cyrus, King of Persia, that he made a proclamation throughout all his kingdom, and put it also in writing, saying:

PROCLAMATION

"Thus saith Cyrus, King of Persia, the Lord God of heaven hath given me all the kingdoms of the earth, and he hath charged me to build him an house at Jerusalem, which is in Judah. Who is there among you of all his people? His God be with him, and let him go up to Jerusalem, which is in Judah, and build the house of the Lord God of Israel, which is in Jerusalem."

Captain of the Host—What say you to the proclamation? Are you willing to go up to Jerusalem?

Principal Sojourner (consulting candidates). — Yes, we are willing to go, but we have no pass-word whereby to make ourselves known to the brethren when we get there. What shall we say to them?

Captain of the Host reads verses 13 and 14 of the third chapter of Exodus:

"And Moses said unto God, Behold! when I come unto the children of Israel, and shall say unto them, The God of your fathers hath sent me unto you, and they shall say to me, What is his name? What shall I say to them?

"And God said unto Moses, I AM THAT I AM: and thus thou shalt say unto the children of Israel, I AM hath sent me unto you."

We were directed to use the words, "I AM THAT I AM," as a pass-word.

Principal Sojourner—We will go up. Companions, you will follow me; our pass-word is, I AM THAT I AM.

As they enter the Chapter, they again pass under the Living Arch.

Principal Sojourner—Stoop low, brethren. He that humbleth himself shall be exalted.

On one side of the hall or Chapter, the Living Arch is formed, as before described; on the other side is what is called the rugged road. This is generally made of blocks and logs of wood, old chairs, benches, &c.

The companions who form the Living Arch press harder on the candidates each time they go through, and they now go through three times. While passing through, the Principal Sojourner says:

Principal Sojourner—This is the way many great and good men have travelled before you, never deeming it derogatory to their dignity to level themselves with the fraternity. I have often travelled this road from Babylon to Jerusalem, and generally find it rough and rugged. However, I think I never saw it much smoother than it is at the present time.

The candidates, after passing the Living Arch, stumble over the rugged road, and arrive again at the entrance of the arch.

Principal Sojourner—Companions, here is a very difficult and dangerous place ahead, which lies directly in our way. Before we attempt to pass it, we must kneel down and pray. (Reads Psalm CXLI.)

"Lord, I cry unto thee; make haste unto me; give ear unto my voice.

"Let my prayer be set forth before thee as incense, and the lifting up of my hands as the evening sacrifice.

"Set a watch, O Lord, before my mouth; keep the door of my lips.

"Incline not my heart to any evil thing, to practice wicked works with men that work iniquity.

"Let the righteous smite me; it shall be a kindness: and let him reprove me; it shall be an excellent oil.

"Mine eyes are unto thee, O God the Lord: in thee is my trust; leave not my soul destitute.

"Keep me from the snare which they have laid before me, and the gins of the workers of iniquity.

"Let the wicked fall into their own nets, whilst that I withal escape."

The candidates rise and again pass under the Living Arch and over the rugged road. They then kneel again.

Principal Sojourner—Let us pray. (Reads from text-book Psalm CXLII.)

"I cried unto the Lord with my voice; with my voice unto the Lord did I make my supplication," &c.

They then pass round the third time as before, when the candidates again kneel.

Principal Sojourner reads Psalm CXLIII. from the text-book:

"Hear my prayer, O Lord, give ear to my supplications; in thy faithfulness answer me, and in thy righteousness," &c.

Principal Sojourner—We have now arrived in sight of the ruins of the old Temple, near the outer veil of the Tabernacle.

The veils are now pushed apart to admit the candidates, but as soon as they enter, the veils are closed again, and the officers (except the Principal Sojourner) take their seats.

Principal Sojourner makes an alarm by stamping nine times on the floor, which brings out the Master from the First Veil. (See Note O, Appendix.)

Master of First Veil—Who comes there? Who dares approach this outer Veil of our sacred Tabernacle? Who are you?

Principal Sojourner—Three weary travellers from Babylon.

Master of First Veil—What are your intentions?

Principal Sojourner—We have come to assist in the noble and glorious work of rebuilding the house of the Lord, without the hope of fee or reward. (See Note M, Appendix.)

Master of First Veil—How do you expect to enter here?

Principal Sojourner—By a pass-word that we received in Babylon.

Master of First Veil—Give it to me.

Principal Sojourner—I AM THAT I AM.

Master of First Veil—The pass is right. You have my permission to enter.

The candidates now enter the First Veil, when the bandages are removed from their eyes.

Master of First Veil—You surely could not have come thus far unless you were three Most Excellent Masters; but farther you cannot go without my words, sign, and word of exhortation. My words are Shem, Ham, and Japhet; my sign is this (holding out a cane), in imitation of one given by God to Moses, when he commanded him to cast his rod upon the ground thus (casting down the cane), and it became a serpent; but putting forth his hand

and taking it up by the tail, it became a rod in his hand as before. My word of exhortation is explanatory of this sign, and is to be found in the writings of Moses, viz.: the first verses of the fourth chapter of Exodus. (See Note N, Appendix.)

"And the Lord said unto Moses, What is that in thy hand? And he said, A rod. And the Lord said, Cast it on the ground; and he cast it, and it became a serpent, and Moses fled from before it," &c.

FIG. 83

SIGN OF THE MASTER OF THE FIRST VEIL

Principal Sojourner—Companions, we have passed the first guard, and will make an alarm at the Second Veil. (Stamps on the floor, as before)

Master of Second Veil—Who comes there? Who dares approach this Second Veil of our sacred Tabernacle?

Principal Sojourner—Three weary sojourners from Babylon, who have come to assist in rebuilding the house of the Lord, without the hope of fee or reward.

Master of Second Veil—How do you expect to enter the Second Veil?

Principal Sojourner—By the words, sign, and word of exhortation of the Master of the First Veil.

Master of Second Veil—Give them.

Principal Sojourner—Shem, Ham, and Japhet. (Gives the sign of casting down a cane and taking it up by the end, as before explained.)

Master of Second Veil—They are right. You have my permission to enter the Second Veil.

The candidates, led by the Principal Sojourner, pass in.

FIG. 34   FIG. 35

SIGN OF THE MASTER OF THE   SIGN OF THE MASTER OF THE
SECOND VEIL   THIRD VEIL

Master of Second Veil—Three Most Excellent Masters you must have been, or thus far you could not have come; but farther you cannot go without my words, sign, and word of exhortation. My words are Shem, Japhet, and Adoniram; my sign is this: (thrusting his hand in his bosom); it is in imitation of one given by God to Moses, when He commanded him to thrust his hand into his bosom, and, taking it out, it became as leprous as snow. My word of exhortation is explanatory of this sign, and is found in the writings of Moses, viz., fourth chapter of Exodus:

"And the Lord said unto Moses, Put now thine hand into thy

bosom. And he put his hand into his bosom; and when he took it out, behold, his hand was leprous as snow," &c.

Principal Sojourner—Companions, we will pass on, and make an alarm at the Third Veil. (Stamps nine times.)

Master of the Third Veil—Who comes there? Who dares approach this Third Veil of our sacred Tabernacle?

Principal Sojourner—Three weary sojourners from Babylon, who have come to assist in the rebuilding of the house of the Lord, without the hope of fee or reward.

Master of Third Veil—How do you expect to enter?

Principal Sojourner—By the words, sign, and word of exhortation of the Master of the Second Veil.

Master of Third Veil—Give them.

Principal Sojourner—Shem, Japhet, and Adoniram. (Thrusts his hand into his bosom as Master of Second Veil had done.)

Master of Third Veil—They are right. You can enter the Third Veil.

The candidates enter.

Master of Third Veil (to candidates).—Three Most Excellent Masters you must have been, or thus far you could not have come. But you cannot go farther without my words, signs, and word of exhortation. My words are, Haggai, Joshua, and Zerubbabel. My sign is this: (holds out a tumbler of water, and pours out a little on the floor.) It is in imitation of one given by God to Moses, when he commanded him to pour water upon the dry land, and it became blood. My word of exhortation is explanato y of this sign, and is found in the writings of Moses, viz., the fourth chapter of Exodus:

"And it shall come to pass, if they will not believe in the two former signs, thou shalt take of the water of the river and pour it upon the dry land; and the water shall become blood upon the dry land."

Master of Third Veil—I also present you with the Signet of Truth, which is that of Zerubbabel. (Presents a triangular piece of metal, with ZER-UBBA-BEL engraved on it.)

Principal Sojourner (to candidates). — Companions, we have now passed the Third Veil: let us make an alarm at the Fourth. (Stamps as before.)

Royal Arch Captain—Who comes there? Who dares approach the Fourth Veil of our sacred Tabernacle, where incense burns, day and night, upon the holy altar? Who are you, and what are your intentions?

Principal Sojourner—Three weary sojourners from Babylon, who have come up thus far to aid and assist in the noble and glorious work of rebuilding the house of the Lord, without the hope of fee or reward.

Royal Arch Captain—How do you expect to enter this Fourth Veil of our sacred Tabernacle?

Principal Sojourner—By the words, sign, and word of exhortation of the Master of the Third Veil.

Royal Arch Captain—Give them.

Principal Sojourner—Haggai, Joshua, and Zerubbabel. (Pours a little water from a tumbler, or cup, upon the floor, for the sign.)

Royal Arch Captain—They are right. You have my permission to enter the Fourth Veil.

The Veils are now drawn aside, and the candidates enter amid a dazzling light, and behold the High Priest, King, and Scribe sitting in Grand Council. The light is usually made by igniting gum camphor in an urn upon the altar.

Royal Arch Captain—Three Most Excellent Masters you must have been, or thus far you could not have come. I will present you to the Grand Council. (Stamps his foot nine times.)

High Priest—Who comes here?

Principal Sojourner—Three weary sojourners from Babylon, who have come up thus far to aid and assist in rebuilding the house of the Lord, without the hope of fee or reward.

High Priest—Have you the signet of Zerubbabel?

Principal Sojourner—We have. (Presents the signet given him by Master of Third Veil.)

High Priest takes it, and reads from the second chapter of Haggai:

"In that day will I take thee, O Zerubbabel, my servant, the son of Shealtiel, saith the Lord, and will make thee a signet: for I have chosen thee."

High Priest (to King, showing him the signet).—Companion, are you satisfied that this is the signet of Zerubbabel?

King (taking the signet, and scrutinizing it).—I am satisfied, Most Excellent, that it is.

High Priest (showing signet to Scribe).—Companion Scribe, think you this is the true signet of Zerubbabel?

Scribe (looking shrewdly at it).—I am satisfied that it is, Most Excellent.

High Priest (drawing signet across his forehead, in imitation of the penalty, see Fig. 36).—Signet of Truth, and Holiness to the Lord!

The King and the Scribe, each in turn, puts his hand to his forehead, repeating—Holiness to the Lord.

High Priest (to candidates).—It is the opinion of the Grand

Council, that you have presented the true signet of Zerubbabel. But, owing to difficulties having arisen from the introduction of strangers among the workmen, none are allowed to undertake in the noble and glorious work, but the true descendants of the twelve tribes. It is necessary you should be very particular in tracing your genealogy. Who are you, and what are your intentions?

Principal Sojourner—We are your own kindred, the descendants of those noble families of Giblemites, who wrought so hard at the building of the first Temple. We have been regularly initiated as Entered Apprentice Masons, passed to the Degree of Fellow Craft, raised to the sublime Degree of Master Mason, advanced to the honorary Degree of Mark Master, presided as Master in the chair, and at the completion and dedication of the Temple were acknowledged as Most Excellent Masters. We were present at its destruction by Nebuchadnezzar, and by him were carried away captives to Babylon; where we remained servants to him and his successors until the reign of Cyrus, King of Persia, by whose proclamation we were liberated, and have come up thus far to aid and assist in the noble and glorious work of rebuilding the house of the Lord, without the hope of fee or reward.

High Priest—Let the captives be unbound, and brought to light. Companion King, I think we had better employ these sojourners. They look like good hardy men; just such men as we want about the building. What say you?

King—It is my opinion, Most Excellent, that they are very expert workmen. I wish they might be examined.

High Priest—What is your opinion, Companion Scribe?

Scribe—If they can satisfy us they are Free Masons, I shall be in favor of employing them immediately.

High Priest—You say you are Entered Apprentice Masons. Satisfy the Grand Council.

The three candidates give the signs of Entered Apprentice. (See Figs. 1 and 2, pp. 17, 18.)

High Priest (to King and Scribe). —Companions, are you satisfied?

The King bows gracefully, and the Scribe answers, We are satisfied, Most Excellent.

High Priest (to candidates).—The Grand Council are satisfied that you are Entered Apprentice Masons. Have you been advanced to the Fellow Craft's Degree?

Candidates give the Fellow Craft signs (see Figs. 3 and 4, p. 17), when the High Priest asks his companions of the Grand Council if they are satisfied, as before, and then informs the candidates that the Grand Council approves them as true Fellow Crafts, &c.

The same questions and answers are given in like manner as to each Degree, up to and including that of Most Excellent Master, and the candidates give all the signs of those Degrees to the Grand Council in detail.

High Priest (after consultation with the King and Scribe).—Companions, we are satisfied that you are three worthy Most Excellent Masters. As such, we will employ you on the Temple. What part of the work will you undertake?

Principal Sojourner—We will take any service, however servile or dangerous, for the sake of forwarding so great and noble an undertaking.

High Priest (to Royal Arch Captain).—You will furnish them with the working tools, and direct them to repair to the northeast corner of the ruins of the old Temple, with orders to remove the rubbish, preparatory to laying the foundation of the new Temple. Advise them to carefully preserve every thing of service to the craft that falls in their way, and bring it to the Grand Council.

The candidates are presented, one with a pickaxe, one with a crow, and the other with a shovel, which are generally made of wood, and kept for the purpose in the Lodge or Chapter.

WORKING TOOLS OF A ROYAL ARCH MASON

Principal Sojourner (to the candidates).—Follow me.

Each candidate shoulders his working tools and follows the Principal Sojourner, going single file to a corner of the room where a quantity of blocks or bricks are scattered around. These they stir up a little, when they come to a ring in a trap-door, which they pull up, and find it shaped like a keystone of an arch. Each one examines it, and then looks down the trap, when the Principal Sojourner suggests that it be at once taken up to the Grand Council. He then leads the candidates back.

High Priest—Companion King, have you further business to lay before this Grand Council?

King—I have nothing, Most Excellent.

High Priest (to Scribe).—Have you any thing, worthy companion?

Scribe—I know of nothing, Most Excellent.

High Priest—I know of nothing, unless the workmen from the ruins have articles for inspection. The workmen will please come forward and give an account of their labors.

Principal Sojourner—Most Excellent, in pursuance of orders of this Grand Council. we repaired to the ruins and commenced our labors. After laboring several days, we discovered what seemed a rock, but on striking it with a crow it gave a hollow sound, and upon closer examination we discovered in it an iron ring, by help of which we succeeded in removing it from its place, when we found it to be the keystone of an arch, and through the aperture there appeared to be an immense vault, curiously arched. We have brought this keystone up, that it may be examined by the Grand Council.

High Priest—You will present it.

Principal Sojourner presents the keystone, or trap.

High Priest (looking closely at it).—Companion King, this is a very valuable discovery indeed. It must be a keystone of a Mark Master Mason.

King—I think that is the stone wrought by our Grand Master, Hiram Abiff.

High Priest—What think you of it, Companion Scribe?

Scribe—It is undoubtedly the stone wrought by our Grand Master, Hiram Abiff.

High Priest (drawing the keystone across his forehead, and giving the sign).—The keystone of a Mark Master! Holiness to the Lord.

King and Scribe do and say the same.

High Priest (to candidates).—This is a very valuable discovery indeed. No doubt it will lead to some important treasure, of inestimable value to the craft. Are you willing to pursue your labors, and endeavor to penetrate this secret vault?

Principal Sojourner (after consulting candidates).—We are, even to the risk of our lives.

High Priest—Go; and may the God of your fathers be with you. Preserve every thing that falls in your way.

The Principal Sojourner returns with the candidates to the place where they lifted the trap, and they there consult together as to who shall descend into the vault. One of the candidates agreeing to go, they put a rope seven times around his body, leaving two long ends.[1]

---

[1] Candidates at the present day usually descend the vault by means of a ladder.

Principal Sojourner (to candidate who is about to descend).—Companion, it is necessary you should take a little precaution. Should you wish to descend still lower, pull the rope in your left hand: if you wish to ascend, pull that in your right hand.

Two companions take hold of each end of the rope, letting the candidate down eight or ten feet, to another trap-door, where he finds three small trying squares; and, giving the signal of ascending, is drawn up.[1]

Each candidate taking a square, they repair to the Grand Council. As they present themselves, the High Priest reads the following passage from the fourth chapter of Zechariah:

"This is the word of the Lord unto Zerubbabel, saying, Not by might, nor by power, but by my spirit. Who art thou, O great mountain? Before Zerubbabel thou shalt become a plain, and he shall bring forth the headstone thereof with shoutings, crying, Grace, grace unto it. Moreover, the word of the Lord came unto me, saying, The hands of Zerubbabel have laid the foundation of this house; his hands shall also finish it; and thou shalt know that the Lord of hosts hath sent me unto you. For who hath despised the day of small things? For they shall rejoice, and shall see the plummet in the hand of Zerubbabel with those seven."

High Priest (to the King).—Companions, have you any further business for the Grand Council?

King—I have nothing, Most Excellent.

High Priest (to Scribe).—Have you any thing, worthy companion?

Scribe—Nothing, Most Excellent.

High Priest—I know of nothing, unless the workmen from the ruins have something for our inspection.

Principal Sojourner—We have examined the secret vault, Most Excellent, and here is what we have found in it. (Presenting the three trying squares.)

High Priest (drawing one of the squares across his forehead).—The jewels of our ancient Grand Masters, King Solomon, Hiram, King of Tyre, and Hiram Abiff! Holiness to the Lord.

The King and the Scribe each take one and imitate the High Priest.

High Priest (to candidates).—Are you willing to continue your labors, and still further penetrate this secret vault?

---

[1] A candidate is said to be EXALTED, when he receives the Degree of Holy Royal Arch, the Seventh in York Masonry. Exalted means *elevated* or *lifted up*, and is applicable both to a peculiar ceremony of the Degree, and to the fact that this Degree, in the rite in which it is practised, constitutes the summit of ancient Masonry. —*Lexicon*.

Principal Sojourner—We are, even to the risk of our lives.

High Priest—Go; and may the God of your fathers be with you; and remember that your labors shall not go unrewarded.

The Principal Sojourner leads the candidates back as before, and winds the rope round one of them, who is let down the trap, still further down than before, where he finds the Ark, when he gives the signal and is drawn up.

The party immediately return to the Grand Council, two of them carrying the Ark, where they present themselves in the same manner as before, and the High Priest directs them to come forward and give an account of their labors.

Principal Sojourner—Most Excellent, in pursuance of your orders, we repaired to the secret vault, and let down one of our companions. The sun at this time was at its meridian height, the rays of which enabled him to discover a small box, or chest, standing on a pedestal, curiously wrought, and overlaid with gold. On discovering it, he involuntarily found his hand raised in this position (giving the sign as shown in Fig. 36), to guard his eyes from the intense light and heat reflected from it. The air becoming offensive, he gave the signal for ascending, and was immediately drawn out. We have brought this chest up for the examination of the Grand Council.

High Priest (looking with surprise at the Ark).—Companion King, this is the Ark of the Covenant of God.

King (looking at it).—It is undoubtedly the true Ark of the Covenant, Most Excellent.

Scribe (looking at the Ark).—That is also my opinion.

High Priest (taking the Ark).—Let us open it, and see what valuable treasure it may contain. (Opens the Ark, and takes out a book.)

High Priest (to King).—Companion, here is a very ancient-looking book; what can it be? Let us read in it. (Reads first three verses of first chapter of Genesis:)

"In the beginning, God created the heaven and the earth," &c.

After reading these verses, the High Priest turns over to Deuteronomy XXXI., and reads from the 24th to the 26th verses, as follows:

"And it came to pass, when Moses had made an end of writing the words of this law in a book, until they were finished, that Moses commanded the Levites, which bare the Ark of the Covenant of the Lord, saying, Take this book of the law, and put it in the side of the Ark of the Covenant of the Lord your God, that it may be there for a witness against thee."

The High Priest then turns back to Exodus XXV., and reads the 21st verse, as follows:

EMBLEMS OF THE ROYAL ARCH DEGREE

1. The Keystone. 2. The Three Jewels of the Ancient Grand Masters. 3. The Ark. 4. Book of the Law. 5. Pot of Manna. 6. Aaron's Rod. 7. The Key. 8. Grand Omnific Word.

"And thou shalt put the mercy-seat above upon the Ark; and in the Ark thou shalt put the testimony that I shall give thee."

High Priest—This is a book of the law—long lost, but now found. Holiness to the Lord. (He repeats this again, twice.)

King—A book of the law—long lost, but now found. Holiness to the Lord!

Scribe repeats the same.

High Priest (to candidates).—You now see that the world is indebted to Masonry for the preservation of this sacred volume. Had it not been for the wisdom and precaution of our ancient brethren, this, the only remaining copy of the law, would have been destroyed at the destruction of Jerusalem.[1]

---

[1] The foundations of the Temple were opened and cleared from the accumulation of rubbish, that a level site might be procured for the commencement of the building. While engaged in excavations for this purpose, *three fortunate sojourners* are said to have discovered our ancient stone of foundation, which had been deposited in the secret crypt by Wisdom, Strength, and Beauty, to prevent the communication of ineffable secrets to profane or unworthy persons. The discovery having been communicated to the prince, priest, and prophet of the Jews, the stone was adopted as the chief corner-stone of the re-edified building; and thus became, in a new and expressive sense, the type of a more excellent dispensation. An avenue was also accidentally discovered, supported by seven pairs of pillars, perfect and entire, which, from their situation, had escaped the fury of the flames that had consumed the Temple, and the desolation of war which had destroyed the city. This secret vault, which had been built by Solomon as a secure depository for certain valuable secrets, that would inevitably have been lost without some such expedient for their preservation, communicated by a subterranean avenue with the King's palace; but at the destruction of Jerusalem, the entrance having been closed by the rubbish of falling buildings, it had been now discovered by the appearance of a *keystone among the foundations* of the Sanctum Sanctorum. A careful inspection was then made, and the invaluable secrets were placed in safe custody.—*Historical Landmarks,* vol. II. p. 434.

In preparing the foundations, as we are told by the Jewish Rabbins, the workmen discovered a subterranean vault or cavity, supported by seven pairs of pillars supporting so many arches. This vault, at the destruction of Jerusalem, having been filled with the rubbish of the building, escaped observation, and was indicated at the present period by the discovery of *a keystone among the foundations.* The Rabbins add, that Josiah, foreseeing the destruction of the Temple, commanded the Levites to deposit the Ark of the Covenant in this vault, where it was found by some of Zerubbabel's workmen. But there is no ground for this belief; for if the secret of the vault had been known to Josiah, it must have been known also to his idolatrous predecessors, who would doubtless have plundered it of its valuable contents, and exposed them to the world, in contempt of the true God to whom they referred, and whom these degenerate monarchs had wholly renounced. It is much more probable, that in the latter years of Solomon, when he had almost forgotten God, his visits to this vault were discontinued, and the entrance being curiously concealed among the caverns underneath his palace, the secret died with him, and the communication was forever closed. It is certain, however, if the tradition of this vault be correct, that *the Ark of the Covenant was not found in it;* for it was one of the invaluable gifts of God which the second Temple did not contain, and consequently it could not have been preserved by Josiah.—*Historical Landmarks,* vol. II. p. 436.

High Priest (taking a little pot out of the Ark).—Companion King, what can this be? a pot of manna? We will read in the book of the law, and see what that says: (Reads, *Exodus* XVI. 32-34.)

"And Moses said, This is the thing which the Lord commandeth: Fill an omer of the manna to be kept for your generations, that they may see the bread wherewith I have fed you in the wilderness, when I brought you forth from the land of Egypt. And Moses said unto Aaron, Take a pot, and put an omer full of manna therein, and lay it up before the Lord, to be kept for your generations. As the Lord commanded Moses, so Aaron laid it up before the testimony, to be kept for a token."

High Priest—A Pot of Manna! Holiness to the Lord!

King—A Pot of Manna! Holiness to the Lord!

Scribe repeats the same.

High Priest—Companions, we read in the book of the law, that he that overcometh, will I give to eat of the hidden manna. Come forward, Companions, you are entitled to it. (Each one receives a small lump of sugar.) But how it came deposited here, we cannot now particularly speak. You must go higher in Masonry before you can know.

The High Priest looks again into the Ark, and finds a stick with some buds upon it, which he shows to the King and Scribe, and after a consultation, they decide that it is Aaron's Rod, and the fact is thus proclaimed in the same manner as the discovery of the manna.

High Priest then reads the following passage, Numbers XVII. 10:

"And the Lord said unto Moses, Bring Aaron's rod again before the testimony, to be kept for a token."

And also, Hebrews IX. 2-5:

"For there was a tabernacle made: the first, wherein was the candlesticks, and the table, and the shew-bread, which is called the sanctuary: and after the second veil, the tabernacle, which is called the Holiest of all; which had the golden censer, and the ark of the covenant, overlaid round about with gold; wherein was the golden pot that had manna; and Aaron's rod, that budded, and the tables of the covenant; and over it the cherubim of glory, shadowing the mercy seat; of which we cannot now speak particularly."

Looking again into the Ark, the High Priest takes out four pieces of paper, which he examines closely, consults with the

King and Scribe, and then puts together, so as to show a *key* to the ineffable characters of this Degree:

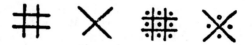

KEY TO THE INEFFABLE CHARACTERS

The key to the ineffable characters, or Royal Arch Cipher, alluded to above, consists of right angles, in various situations, with the addition of a dot. By transposition, it forms twenty-six distinct characters, corresponding with the twenty-six letters of the English alphabet. There are two methods of combining these characters for secret correspondence. One method is to call the first sign, , *a*; the second, , *b*; the third, , *c*; and so on, reading from left to right, thus:

The second way to read the alphabet is as follows:

The upper left angle without a dot is *a*; the same with a dot is *b*, &c.

High Priest then reads Exodus VI. 2, 3:

"And God spake unto Moses, and said unto him, I am the Lord: and I appeared unto Abraham, unto Isaac, and unto Jacob, by the name of God Almighty; but by my name Jehovah was I not known to them."

After examining the Key, he proceeds to read, by the aid of it, the characters on the four sides of the Ark.

High Priest (reading first side).—Deposited in the year three thousand. Second side—By Solomon, King of Israel. Third side —Hiram, King of Tyre, and Hiram Abiff. Fourth side—For the good of Masonry, generally, but the Jewish nation in particular.[1]

High Priest (to candidates).—Companions, here are three mysterious words, in a triangular form, upon the Ark, which, when first found, were covered with three squares, the jewels of our three ancient Grand Masters; and from this circumstance, we supposed it to be the long-lost Master Mason's word; and, on applying our Key to it, it proved our suspicions to be correct. It is the name of Deity in three languages, viz., Chaldaic, Hebrew and Syriac, which is the long-lost Master Mason's word, or Logos, and has now become the Grand Omnific Royal Arch word.

It is the divine Logos, or Word, to which reference is had in John (I. 1-5):

"In the beginning was the word (Logos), and the word was with God, and the word was God; the same was in the beginning with God: all things were made by him, and without him was not any thing made that was made; in him was life, and the life was the light of men: and the light shineth in darkness, and the darkness comprehended it not."

This word was anciently written only in these sacred characters, and thus preserved from one generation to another. It was lost by the death of Hiram Abiff, was found again at the building of the Temple, and will now be given to you; and you will remember the manner you receive it, and that you have sworn never to give it to others except in that particular manner.

The candidates, instructed by the Principal Sojourner, now learn the Grand Omnific Royal Arch Word, as follows:

Each one takes hold with his right hand of the right wrist of his companion on the left, and with his left hand takes hold of the left wrist of his companion on the right. Each one then

---

[1] The author of *Ahiman Rezon* has stated that he could convey his mind to an ancient Mason in the presence of a modern Mason, without the latter knowing whether either of them were Masons. He further asserted that he was able, with a few Masonic implements, i. e., two squares and a common gavel or hammer, to convey any word or sentence of his own, or the immediate dictations of a stranger, to a skilful and intelligent Freemason of the ancient order, without speaking, writing, or noise; and that to any distance, when the parties can see each other, and at the same time be able to distinguish squares from circles. This Masonic system of cipher-writing is now well understood.—*Origin of the English Royal Arch*, p. 42.

places his right foot forward with the hollow in front, so that the toe touches the heel of his companion on the right. This is called "three times three;" that is, three right feet forming a triangle, three left hands forming a triangle, and three right hands forming a triangle. They balance in the same manner, and then, with hands raised, repeat the words Jah-buh-lun, Je-hovah, G-o d, at low breath, as described before. (See pp. 224-25, Fig. 32.)[1]

[1] The WORD of the Royal Arch Degree, as worked in England, is *Jao-Bul-On.*

"Macrobius, in his Saturnalia (lib. I. 18), says that it was an admitted axiom among the heathen, that the triliteral JAH, or rather IAΩ, was the sacred name of the Supreme God. And the Clarian oracle, which was of unknown antiquity, being asked which of the deities was named IAΩ, answered in these memorable words:

"'The initiated are bound to conceal the mysterious secrets. Learn thou, that IAΩ, is the Great God Supreme, who ruleth over all.'

"Now it so happens, that in the gems of the early Christians we find these very letters, IAΩ, which are an abbreviation of the name of JEHOVAH, used as a monogram to express the name of the Saviour of mankind, who was thus represented as existing before time was, and shall exist when time shall be no more. It was first adopted by the Eastern Church, and signified *Ιησους, Αλφα Ομεγα,* Jesus, Alpha Omega, or in other words: Jesus, the First and the Last."—*The Insignia of the Royal Arch,* p. 82.

The Royal Arch Word to have been perfectly in keeping with the Degree, and with the general construction of Masonry, should have been a triad, not only of syllables, but also of letters. Our transatlantic brethren have seen it in its true light; but they have corrected the error unlearnedly. It ought to have been, if the principle of its construction be allowed, to be orthodox:

Syriac	*Chaldee*	*Hindoo*

The Insignia of the Royal Arch, p. 84.

That is to say, instead of JAO-BUL-ON, or JAH-BUH-LUN, Dr. Oliver suggests:

Syriac	*Chaldee*	*Hindoo*
JAO	BEL	AUN
or	or	or
JAH	BUL	AUM

For at page 15 of *The Insignia,* he writes thus:

"But the Royal Arch Degree is founded on the number *three,* and therefore each member of the word ought to have been triliteral. . . . Among the Syrians, the Chaldeans, the Phœnicians and others, the ineffable name of the Deity was Bel, Bal, Bul, Baal, or Belin. . . . Again, the Egyptians and Hindoos reverenced On or Om, i. e., Aun, or Aum, as the name of their chief Deity."

And vide *Historical Landmarks,* vol. II. p. 549:

"One says it was Jau, another thinks it was Jaoth, a third, Java; others, Juba, Jao, Jah, Jehovah, and Jove. In a word, the letters of the name are perishable, and the pronunciation of little moment; but the Being himself is ineffable, incomprehensible, and worthy of our utmost veneration. He was called by the Romans Jove, or Jah; by the Chaldeans, the Phœnicians, and the Celtæ, Bel or Bul; and by the Indians, Egyptians, and Greeks, Om or On."

The signs of this Degree are now given to the candidates, as follows:

First, raise the right hand to the forehead, the hand and arm horizontal, the thumb toward the forehead; draw it briskly across the forehead, and drop it perpendicularly by the side. This constitutes the duegard and sign of this Degree, and refers not only to the penalty of the obligation, but alludes also to the manner in which the brother who descended into the vault, and found the Ark, found his hands involuntarily placed, to protect his head

FIG. 86   FIG. 87

ROYAL ARCH DUEGARD AND SIGN   ROYAL ARCH GRAND HAILING SIGN [1]

from the rays of the meridian sun. (See Fig. 36.) This sign must be given to the High Priest, upon entering and retiring from a Chapter.

High Priest (placing crowns upon the heads of candidates).— Companions, you are now invested with all the important secrets

[1] The grand hailing sign is made by locking the fingers of both hands together, and carrying them to the top of the head, the palms upward. Then let them drop to the sides.

of this Degree, and crowned and received as worthy Companions Royal Arch Masons.

The High Priest then reads to them from a book the charge in this Degree, informing them that the Degree owes its origin to Zerubbabel and his associates, who rebuilt the Temple by order of Cyrus, King of Persia. He likewise informs them that the discovery of the secret vault and the inestimable treasures, with the long-lost word, actually took place in the manner represented in conferring this Degree, and that it is the circumstance upon which the Degree is principally founded.

The initiation being over, the High Priest begins the closing lecture, which is a repetition, by questions and answers, of the opening of a Chapter, and the advancement of a companion of this Degree. It begins as follows:

High Priest (to Captain of the Host).—Are you a Royal Arch Mason?

Captain—I am that I am.

High Priest—How shall I know you to be a Royal Arch Mason?

Captain of Host—By three times three.

High Priest—Where were you made a Royal Arch Mason?

Captain of the Host—In a just and legally constituted Chapter of Royal Arch Masons, consisting of Most Excellent High Priest, King and Scribe, Captain of the Host, Principal Sojourner, Royal Arch Captain, and the three Grand Masters of the Veils, assembled in a room or place representing the Tabernacle erected by our ancient brethren, near the ruins of King Solomon's Temple.

The High Priest continues his questions as to the station and duties of each officer of the Chapter, and every particular relative to the organization thereof, the initiation or advancement of candidates, &c. The Captain of the Host rehearses or describes the whole precisely as we have given it. These closing lectures are intended to perfect members in the full understanding of each Degree.

After the lecture, the Chapter is closed in the same manner as the opening, up to the raising of the Living Arch. The companions join hands by threes, in the same manner, and say in concert:

> As we three did agree
>   The Sacred Word to keep—
> As we three did agree
>   The Sacred Word to search;
> So we three do agree
>   To close this Royal Arch.

They then break, and the High Priest reads the following prayer:

"By the wisdom of the Supreme High Priest may we be directed, by his strength may we be enabled, and by the beauty of virtue may we be incited to perform the obligations here enjoined upon us, to keep inviolable the mysteries here unfolded to us, and invariably to practise all those duties out of the Chapter which are inculcated in it."

Companions—So mote it be. Amen.

High Priest—I now declare this Chapter of Royal Arch Masons closed.[1]

It is generally conceded by Masonic writers, that ancient Masonry closes with the Royal Arch. In an edition of "The Illustrations of Masonry," by Mr. Preston, published in London, 1829, the editor, Mr. Oliver, observes:

"All Degrees beyond the Royal Arch ought to be carefully separated from genuine Masonry, as they are mostly founded on vague and uncertain traditions, which possess not the shadow of authority to recommend them to our notice."[2]

---

[1] At my first exaltation, I was taught to believe it an ancient degree; but I confess, that even at that period I entertained considerable doubts on the point. The Degree is too incongruous to be of any great antiquity. It exhibits too many evidences of modern construction to be received with implicit credence as a ceremony practised by the ancient Dionysiacs, or even the more modern colleges of Freemasons, or confraternities of the Middle Ages. The earliest mention of it in England which I can find, is in the year 174⁰, just one year after the trifling alteration, sanctioned by the modern Grand Lodge, already mentioned.—*Origin of the English Royal Arch*, pp. 19, 20.

[2] The fact is, the grand omnific *(all-creating) lost word*, it will be seen in the sequel, was eventually found in a vault under the ruins of Solomon's Temple; and the difficulty was, *rationally* to account for the manner in which it got there. This, therefore, is the grand object of the *Select Master's Degree;* and, at the same time, so to locate the word as symbolically to represent its archetype, the sun *lost* in the inferior hemisphere. For this purpose a history of the order was manufactured by its founders, of which the following is a sketch:

"The three Grand Masters, at the building of the Temple, entered into a solemn agreement not to confer the Master's Degree until the Temple should be completed; that all three must be present when it should be conferred, and if either should be taken away by death prior to the finishing of the Temple, the Master's Degree should be lost.

"After this *wise* arrangement, lest the knowledge of the arts and sciences, together with the patterns and valuable models which were contained in the Temple, should be lost, they agreed to build a *secret vault* under ground, leading from Solomon's most retired apartment, a *due west course*, and ending under the *sanctum sanctorum* of the Temple, to be divided into *nine separate arches*. The ninth arch was to be the place for holding the grand council, and also for a deposit of a true copy of all those things which were *contained in the sanctum sanctorum above.*

"After the ninth arch was completed, the three Grand Masters deposited therein those things which were important to the craft, such as the Ark of the Covenant, a pot of manna, the rod of Aaron, the book of the law, etc.

The additional Degrees, including those considered legitimate, amount to upward of fifty. These are founded partly upon astronomical principles, agreeing with the ancient worship of the Egyptians, and partly upon the Hebrew and Christian doctrines.

It may be remarked in general, that many of the degrees of knights are founded on the Christian knighthoods got up in the time of the Crusades, in the twelfth century; and that the ceremonies thereof are an imitation of those superstitious establishments. A former Grand High Priest of the Chapters in the State of New York informs me, that he initiated a French gentleman into the Degree of Knight of Malta, who told him he was a member of the ancient order of that name, and that the ceremonies were very similar.

At the time those old knighthoods were founded, "superstition mingled in every public and private action of life; in the holy wars it sanctified the profession of arms; and the order of chivalry was assimilated in its rights and privileges to the sacred orders of priesthood. The bath and the white garment of the novice were an indecent copy of the regeneration of baptism; his sword, which he offered on the altar, was blessed by the ministers of religion; his solemn reception was preceded by fasts and vigils; and he was created a knight in the name of God, of St. George, and of St. Michael the archangel."—*Rees's Cycl.*

The emblem of the Royal Arch Degree is called the *Triple Tau,* and is a figure consisting of three tau crosses. It was adopted at Chicago, 1859, by the General Grand Chapter of the United States, and is worn printed on all aprons of the Royal Arch Degree.

LECTURE ON THE SEVENTH, OR ROYAL ARCH DEGREE.— SECTION FIRST

Question. Are you a Royal Arch Mason?

Answer. I am that I am.

Q. How shall I know you to be a Royal Arch Mason?

A. By three times three.

Q. Where were you exalted to the most, sublime Degree of a Royal Arch Mason?

"Prior to the completion of the Temple, Grand Master Hiram Abiff was assassinated, and by his death the Master's Word was lost. The two kings were willing to do all in their power to preserve the *Sacred Word,* and as they could not communicate it to any, by reason of the death of Hiram, they agreed to place it in the *secret vault,* that if the other treasures were ever brought to light, the *Word* might be found also."—*Fellows's Inquiry into the Origin, History, and Purport of Freemasonry,* pp. 808, 809.

A. In a regularly and duly constituted Chapter of Royal Arch Masons assembled in a place representing a Tabernacle, erected by our ancient brethren near the ruins of King Solomon's temple.

Q. How many constitute a Chapter of Royal Arch Masons?

A. Nine Regular Royal Arch Masons—consisting of Most Excellent High Priest, Excellent King, and Scribe, Captain of the Host, Principal Sojourner, Royal Arch Captain, and three Masters of the veils.

Q. Who do the three former represent?

A. Those of our ancient brethren who formed the first Most Grand Council at Jerusalem, and held their meetings in a tabernacle.

Q. Who did the three latter represent?

A. Those of our ancient brethren, who directed and brought to light the principal secrets of this Degree, after they had lain buried in darkness from the death of our Grand Master Hiram Abiff, until the erection of the second temple, and as a reward for their zeal, fortitude and attachment to Masonry, were exalted to become the three Grand Masters of the veils.

Q. How many veils were they?

A. Four.

Q. What were their colors?

A. Blue, purple, scarlet and white.

Q. What does blue denote?

A. Friendship, and is the principal color of a Master Mason.

Q. What does purple denote?

A. It being composed of blue and scarlet, it is placed before the first and third veils of the colors, to denote the intimate connection between this most sublime degree, and ancient Craft Masonry.

Q. What does scarlet denote?

A. That fervency and zeal which should actuate all Royal Arch Masons, and is the peculiar color of this Degree.

Q. What does white denote?

A. That purity of life and rectitude of conduct which should govern all those who seek to gain admission into that Sanctum Sanctorum, or Holy of Holies.

Q. To whom do the four veils allude?

A. To the four tribes of the children of Israel, who bore the banners through the wilderness, viz.: Judah, Reuben, Ephraim and Dan, emblematically represented by the strength of the Lion, the intelligence of the Man, the patience of the Ox and the swiftness of the Eagle.

Q. Where were the veils placed?

A. At the outer courts of the tabernacle.

Q. Why there?

A. To serve as a covering for the tabernacle and stations for the guards.

Q. Why were guards stationed there?

A. To take special pains that none pass or repass, except such as were duly qualified, as none were permitted to enter the presence of the Most Excellent High Priest, Excellent King, and Scribe, except the true descendants of the twelve (12) tribes of the children of Israel.

Q. How did the children of Israel make themselves known to the several guards?

A. By the same words and signs given by God to Moses. He was commanded to conduct the children of Israel out of the land of Egypt from the bands of bondage.

SECOND SECTION

Q. Where were you prepared to be exalted to the Most Sublime degree of a Royal Arch Mason?

A. In a room adjoining a regular and duly constituted Chapter of Royal Arch Masons.

Q. How were you prepared.

A. I was divested of my outward apparel, in a working posture, hoodwinked, and a cable-tow seven times around my body, accompanied by two (2) brethren possessed of like qualifications, in which condition we were conducted to the door of the Chapter, where a regular demand was made by seven (7) distinct knocks.

Q. To what do the seven (7) distinct knocks allude?

A. To the seventh Degree of Masonry, it being that upon which I was about to enter.

Q. What was said to you from within?

A. Who comes here?

Q. Your answer?

A. Three worthy brothers (or brethren) who have been duly initiated, passed to the Degree of Fellow Craft, raised to the Sublime Degree of Master Mason, advanced to the Degree of Mark Master Mason, regularly passed the Chair—have been received and acknowledged as Most Excellent Masters, and now wish further promotion in Masonry, by being exalted to the Most Sublime Degree of a Royal Arch Mason.

Q. What were you then asked?

A. If it was an act of my own free will and accord, if I was worthy and well qualified, duly and truly prepared, if I had made suitable proficiencies in the preceding Degree, and was properly vouched for—all of which being answered in the affirmative, I was asked by what further right or benefit I expected to obtain this important privilege.

Q. Your answer?

A. By the benefit of the pass.

Q. Give the pass?

A. Rabboni.

Q. What does it signify?

A. Good Master, or Most Excellent Master.

Q. What was then said to you?

A. We were directed to wait until the Captain of the Host could be informed of our request, and his answer returned.

Q. What was his answer when returned?

A. Let the candidates enter and be received in due and ancient form.

Q. How were you received in a Chapter of Royal Arch Masons?

A. Under a living arch.

Q. Why under a living arch?

A. To imprint upon my mind in the most solemn manner that the principal secrets of this Degree should be communicated only under a living arch.

Q. How were you then disposed of?

A. We were conducted once around the outer courts of the tabernacle, there caused to kneel at the altar and invoke a blessing from Deity.

Q. After invoking a blessing from Deity, how were you then disposed of?

A. We were again conducted around the outer courts of the tabernacle, where we were met by the Captain of the Host, who demanded of us who comes here, and what were our intentions.

Q. Your answer?

A. As at the door.

Q. Of what did the Captain of the Host inform you?

A. That in pursuing our intentions, we should be under the disagreeable necessity of travelling those rough and rugged paths, which all Royal Arch Masons have done before us, but before pursuing further it would be necessary for us to kneel at the altar in due form, and take upon ourselves the solemn oath or obligation of a Royal Arch Mason.

Q. What was that due form?

A. Kneeling upon both knees, both hands covering the Holy Bible, square and compasses, in which due form I took upon myself the solemn oath or obligation of a Royal Arch Mason.

Q. Have you that oath?

A. I have.

Q. Will you give it?

A. I will with your assistance.

Q. Proceed. (I, A. B., etc., etc.)

Q. After the oath how were you then disposed of?

A. We were again conducted around the outer courts of the tabernacle, where was exhibited the symbol of the burning bush.

Q. Why was the symbol of the burning bush exhibited to you at this point of your exaltation?

A. To impress upon my mind in the most solemn manner, that the words and signs following were of divine origin, and as such were regarded sacred by the children of Israel—by them transmitted to their posterity, as words and signs by which they should make themselves known and be distinguished by each other for ever after.

Q. How were you then disposed of?

A. We were again conducted around the outer courts of the tabernacle, where a representation of the destruction of the temple took place.

Q. By whom was it destroyed?

A. By Nebuchadnezzar, King of Babylon, who in the eleventh year of Zedekiah, King of Jerusalem, went up, besieged and took the city, seized on all the holy vessels, together with the two brazen pillars; and the remnant of the people who escaped the sword, he carried away captives to Babylon.

Q. What was the period of their captivity?

A. Seventy (70) years.

Q. By whom were they delivered?

A. By Cyrus, King of Persia, who in the first year of his reign issued his yearly proclamation saying: "Thus says Cyrus, King of Persia," etc., etc. (See Monitor.)

Q. Who did you then represent?

A. Those of our ancient brethren being released from their captivity.

Q. In that case what answer did you make Cyrus, King of Persia?

A. But behold when I come unto the children of Israel, etc., etc. (Monitorial.)

Q. What answer did you receive from the Captain of the Host?

A. I am that I am, I am hath sent me unto you.

Q. Did you pursue your journey?

A. We did, the rough and rugged paths.

Q. What do the rough and rugged paths denote?

A. The sojourning of the children of Israel through the wilderness.

Q. Did you meet with any obstructions?

A. We did, several.

Q. Where did you meet with the first obstruction?

A. At the first veil, where on making the regular demand, we
heard the Master of that veil exclaim, "Who dares approach this
first veil of our sacred tabernacle?" and he, supposing an enemy
to be approaching, hailed his companions, who on being assembled
demanded, "Who comes here?"

Q. Your answer?

A. We are of your own brethren and kin—children of the captivity—descendants of those noble Giblemites, we were received
and acknowledged Most Excellent Masters at the completion and
dedication of the first temple—were present at the destruction of
that temple by Nebuchadnezzar, by whom we were carried captives to Babylon, where we remained servants to him and his successors, until the reign of Cyrus, King of Persia, by whose order
we have been liberated, and have now come up to help, aid, and
assist in rebuilding the house of the Lord, without the hope of
fee or reward.

Q. What were you then asked?

A. By what further reward or benefit we expected to obtain
this important privilege.

Q. Your answer?

A. By the benefit of the pass.

Q. Give it? (I am that I am, I am hath sent me unto you.)

Q. Did this give you admission?

A. It did within the first veil.

Q. What was then said to you?

A. Good men and true you must have been, to have come thus
far to promote so noble and good an undertaking; but further you
cannot go without my word, sign, and word of explanation.

Q. What was the word of the Master of the first veil?

A. I am that I am, I am hath sent you unto us, Shem, Ham, and
Japheth.

Q. What is his sign?

A. It is in imitation of that given by God to Moses when he
was commanded to cast his rod upon the ground, and it became a
serpent.

Q. What was his word of explanation?

A. It was explanatory of the sign as recorded by Moses, and is
as follows. "And Moses answered and said, But behold they will
not believe me, nor hearken unto my voice, for they will say, The

Lord hath not appeared unto thee; and the Lord said unto him, What is that in thine hand, and he said, A rod; and He said, Cast it on the ground. And he cast it on the ground and it became a serpent, and Moses fled from before it; and the Lord said, Put forth thine hand and take it by the tail; and he put forth his hand and caught it, and it become a rod in his hand, that they may believe that the God of their fathers, the God of Abraham, the God of Isaac, and the God of Jacob hath appeared unto thee.

Q. Where did you meet with the next obstruction?

A. At the second veil, where, on making the regular demand, we heard the master of that exclaim as before.

Q. Your answer?

A. As before.

Q. What were you then asked?

A. By what further right or benefit we expected to obtain that important privilege.

Q. Your answer?

A. By the word and sign given us by the master of the first veil.

Q. Did this gain you admission?

A. It did within the second veil.

Q. What was then said to you?

A. Good men and true you must have been, to have come thus far to engage in so noble and glorious an undertaking, but further you cannot go without my word and sign, and word of explanation.

Q. What was the word of the master of the second veil?

A. I am that I am, I am hath sent me unto you, Shem, Ham, and Japheth.

Q. What is his sign?

A. It is in imitation of that given by God to Moses, when he commanded him to put his hand into his bosom, and when he took it out, behold it was as leprous as snow.

Q. What is his word of explanation?

A. It is explanatory of that sign, is recorded by Moses, and is as follows: And the Lord said unto Moses, Put now thine hand into thy bosom, and he put his hand into his bosom, and when he took it out, behold, his hand was leprous as snow. And He said, Put thine hand into thy bosom again, and he put his hand into his bosom again, and plucked it out of his bosom, and behold it was turned again as his other flesh. And it shall come to pass if they will not believe thee, neither hearken to the voice of the first sign, that they will believe the voice of the latter sign.

Q. Where did you meet with the next obstruction?

A. At the third veil, where, on making the regular demand, we heard the master of that veil exclaim as before.

Q. Your answer?

A. As before.

Q. What were you then asked?

A. By what further right or benefit we expected to obtain this important privilege.

Q. Your answer?

A. By the benefit of the word and sign given us by the masters of the first and second veils.

Q. Did they gain you admission?

A. They did within the third veil.

Q. What was then said to you?

A. Good men and true you must have been, to have come thus far to promote so noble and good an undertaking, but further you cannot go without my sign and word of explanation and *signet.*

Q. What was his sign?

A. It is in imitation of that given by God to Moses, when he commanded him to take of the water of the river and pour it upon the dry land.

Q. What is his word of explanation?

A. It is explanatory of that sign, is recorded by Moses, and is as follows: And it shall come to pass if they will not believe also these two signs, neither hearken unto thy voice, that thou shalt take of the water of the river and pour it upon the dry land, and the water which thou takest out of the river shall become blood upon the dry land.

Q. Where did you meet with the next obstruction?

A. At the fourth veil or sanctuary, where on making the regular demand, we heard the Royal Arch Captain exclaim, "Who dares approach the fourth veil or sanctuary, where incense burns upon our holy altar both day and night? Who comes here?"

Q. Your answer?

A. Three worthy sojourners, who have come up to help, aid, and assist in the rebuilding of the house of the Lord, without the hope of fee or reward.

Q. What were you then asked?

A. Whence came you?

Q. Your answer?

A. From Babylon.

Q. Of what were you then informed.

A. That by a degree of the *Grand Council,* then in session, made in consequence of difficulties having arisen by the introduction of strangers among the workmen, none are permitted to enter the presence of the Most Excellent High Priest, Excellent King, and Scribe, while sitting in council, excepting the true descendants of the twelve tribes of the children of Israel; it was therefore necessary that we be more particular in tracing our genealogy, and demanded who we were.

Q. Your answer?

A. We are of your brethren and kin—children of the captivity—we have been received as Most Excellent Masters, and as such have made ourselves known to the several guards, and now wait permission to enter the presence of the Grand Council.

Q. What were you then asked?

A. By what further right or benefit we expected to obtain this important privilege.

Q. Your answer?

A. By the benefit of the words and signs given us by the masters of the first, second and third veils, together with the signet.

Q. What was then said to you?

A. We were directed to wait until the Captain of the Host could be informed of our request and his answer returned.

Q. What answer did he return?

A. Let them be admitted.

Q. By whom were you received?

A. By the Captain of the Host, who conducted us into the presence of the Grand Council, who examined us as to our proficiency in the preceding degree, and expressed satisfaction at our meeting, after which we were asked what part of the work we were willing to undertake.

Q. Your answer?

A. Any part, even the most servile, to promote so noble and glorious an undertaking.

Q. Of what were you then informed?

A. That from the specimens of skill which we had exhibited, the Grand Council had confidence and belief that we were able to undertake any part, even the most difficult, but that it was necessary that some more of the rubbish be removed from the northeast part of the ruins, and they instructed us to observe and preserve everything that we might discover of value, for they had no doubt that there were many valuable monuments of art there which would be essential to the craft.

Q. What followed?

A. The Captain of the Host furnished us with the necessary working tools, and we repaired to the place as directed, where we wrought diligently four days without discovering anything of interest, excepting passing the ruins of several columns of the order of architecture; on the fifth, still pursuing our labors, we experienced that which we at first supposed to be an impenetrable rock, but on my companion striking it with his crow, it reverberated a hollow sound, upon which we redoubled our assiduity, and removing some more of the rubbish, we found it to resemble the top of an arch, in the apex of which was a stone having on it certain characters which by length of time were nearly effaced. Night now drawing on, we repaired with it to the Grand Council.

Q. What was their opinion of the stone?

A. That it was the keystone to the principal arch of King Solomon's Temple, and from the place in which it was found, they had no doubt it would lead to important discoveries; upon which we were asked if we were willing on the morrow to descend the arch in search of them.

Q. Your answer?

A. That the task would be attended with difficulties and dangers, yet we were willing even at the risk of our lives to promote so noble and glorious an undertaking.

Q. What followed?

A. We repaired to the place as before, and removed some more of the rubbish, after which we placed a cable-tow seven times around the body of one of my companions to assist him in descending, and it was agreed, should the place become offensive, either to health or sight, he should swing it to the right as a signal to ascend; but should he wish to descend he should swing it to the left. In this manner he descended and found three squares, which they had no doubt had long been concealed; he gave the signal and ascended, and with them we repaired to the Grand Council.

Q. What was their opinion of the squares?

A. That they were masters' jewels, most probably worn by our ancient Grand Masters, Solomon, King of Israel, Hiram, King of Tyre, and Hiram Abiff, and from the place in which they were found they had no doubt they would lead to still further and more important discoveries, upon which we were asked if willing again to descend the arch in search of the treasures.

Q. Your answer? (As before.)

Q. What followed?

A. We repaired to the place as before, which I descended as before. The sun shone forth with such redoubled splendor that I was enabled to descend; in the eastern-most part thereof was a trunk of curious form, overlaid with gold, having on its top and sides certain mysterious characters; availing myself of this I gave the signal, and ascended; on arriving at the top of the arch I found my hands involuntarily placed in this position to guard my eyes from the intense light and heat that arose therefrom above; with the trunk we repaired to the Grand Council.

Q. What was their opinion of the trunk?

A. That it was the Ark of the Covenant.

Q. What were its contents?

A. A pot, a rod, and a book.

Q. What was their opinion of the pot?

A. That it was the pot of manna, which Moses by divine command, laid up in the side of the ark as a memorial of the miraculous manner in which the children of Israel were supplied with that article of food for forty years in the wilderness.

Q. What was their opinion of the rod?

A. That it was Aaron's rod, that budded and blossomed, and bore fruit in a day, which Moses also, by divine command, laid in the side of the ark as a testimony, to be kept for a token.

Q. What was their opinion of the book?

A. That it was the book of the law in which it is written, I am the Lord, I appeared unto Abraham, unto Isaac and Jacob by the name of God Almighty, but by my great and sacred name was I not known unto them.

Q. What does it contain?

A. A key to the mysterious characters upon its top and sides, by which they found those upon its sides to be the initials of our three ancient Grand Masters, S. K. of I., H. K. of T., and H. Abiff. Those upon its top, the Grand Omnific or Royal Arch word, which we as Royal Arch Masons should never give except in the presence of three Royal Arch Masons, we first agreeing by three times three, and under a living arch.

Q. How were your merits rewarded?

A. The Grand Council descended and invested us with the secrets of the Degree.

Q. How were they communicated?

A. The Grand Omnific Royal Arch word in the presence of three regular Arch Masons, we first agreeing by three times three, and under a living arch.

Q. Have you a sign in this Degree?

A. I have several.

Q. Show me a sign? (Hand to forehead. See sign.)

Q. What is that called?

A. The duegard.

Q. To what does it allude?

A. To the way and manner in which my hands were involuntarily placed on arriving at the arch, to guard my eyes from the intense light and heat that arose therefrom above.

Q. Show me another sign? (Give sign.)

Q. What is that called?

A. The sign.

Q. To what does it allude?

A. To the penalty of my obligation, that I would sooner have my skull struck off than divulge any of the secrets of this Degree unlawfully.

Q. Give me another sign? (Give sign.)

Q. What is that called?

A. The grand hailing sign, or sign of distress of a Royal Arch Mason

Q. To what does it allude?

A. To the additional portion of the penalty of my obligation, that I would sooner have my skull clove off, and have my brain exposed to the scorching rays of a noonday sun, than divulge any of the secrets of this Degree unlawfully.

Q. What are the working tools of a Royal Arch Mason?

A. The pick, spade, and crow.

Q. What does the spade teach us as Royal Arch Masons? (Monitorial.)

Q. What is the use of the crow?

A. It is used by operative masons to describe circles—every part of the circumference of which is equally near and equally distant from its centre; so is every creature whom God hath made equally near and equally dear.

Q. What is the equilateral or perfect triangle upon which the word is formed emblematical of?

A. The three certain attributes of Deity—namely, Omniscience, Omnipotence, and Omnipresence, for as the three equal legs or angles form but one triangle, so the three attributes constitute but one God.

EXTRACTS FROM "A DICTIONARY OF SYMBOLICAL MASONRY, INCLUDING THE ROYAL ARCH DEGREE," BY THE REV. G. OLIVER, D. D.

ACHILLES.—Perhaps some worthy people may stare when we point out Achilles as a Freemason. What! we hear them exclaim, is it possible that that fierce and ferocious man-slayer, nay, man-eater at heart, for he exhibited a strong propensity to cannibalism in longing to have devoured the dead body of Hector —is it possible that he could have been one of our philanthropic society? Yes, we reply, such is the actual fact, and Bonaparte was one, too, in the highest degree. But, if you will not believe Homer, or us, believe your own eyes, if, indeed, you are a Mason. *Ecce signum!* Behold Achilles giving Priam THE HAND, when the latter is supplicating for the body of his slain son:

"Thus having spoken, the old man's *right hand at the wrist*
He grasped, that he might not in any respect be alarmed in mind."

Such is the Masonic and literal translation of the text by that illustrious Grecian and brother, Christopher North; and who will say, now, that Achilles was not a Mason?—*Freemasons' Quarterly Review.*

[According to this, *Brother* Achilles gave *Brother* Priam the Master Mason's Grip, but there is no evidence to show whether they used the word MAH-HAH-BONE, and the Five Points of Fellowship.]

ESSENTIAL SECRETS.—The essential secrets of Masonry consist of nothing more than the signs, grips, pass-words, and tokens, essential to the preservation of the society from the inroads of impostors; together with certain symbolical emblems, the technical terms appertaining to which served as a sort of universal language, by which the members of the fraternity could distinguish each other, in all places and countries where Lodges were instituted. —*Stone.*

EYESIGHT.—He who has been temporarily deprived of his sight is reduced to the condition of a new-born babe, or of one of those unfortunate individuals whose natural infirmity renders the presence of a conductor indispensably necessary; but when there are no outward objects to distract his attention, it is then that with the eye of reflection he probes into the deepest and darkest recesses of his own heart, and discovers his natural imperfections and impurities much more readily than he could possibly have done had he not been deprived of his sight. This short deprivation of sight has kindled in his heart a spark of the brightest and purest flame. . . . We must further admit, that those who have been deprived of their sight, and who have hopes of being restored to it, strive most industriously and diligently to obtain it; that they have no greater desire, and that *they will most readily pledge themselves to do all that can be required of them*, in order to obtain that inestimable blessing.

A man who has been deprived of his sight may be introduced into places where he is surrounded by the strangest and the rarest objects, *without a possibility of his becoming a traitor*. At the same time, those who are in possession of their sight cannot feel the care of their guides so much as those who are hoodwinked, and who feel that without the constant attention of their conductors they would be much more helpless than they now are; but, however many proofs of attention and care they may receive, there is still something left to wish for; and to the question, What is your chief desire? the answer will ever assuredly be, "Light." —*Gadicke*.

FIVE POINTS OF FELLOWSHIP.—The five points of fellowship were thus illustrated in the lectures used by the Athol Masons of the last century:

1. When the necessities of a brother call for my support, I will be ever ready to lend him a helping hand to save him from sinking, if I find him worthy thereof.

2. Indolence shall not cause my footsteps to halt, nor wrath to turn them aside; but, forgetting every selfish consideration, I will be ever swift of foot to save, help, and execute benevolence to a fellow-creature in distress, but more particularly to a brother Mason.

3. When I offer up my ejaculations to Almighty God, I will remember my brother's welfare, even as my own; for as the voice of babes and sucklings ascends to the throne of grace, so, most assuredly, will the breathings of a fervent heart ascend to the mansions of bliss.

4. A brother's secret, delivered to me as such, I will keep as I would my own, because, if I betray the trust which has been reposed in me, I might do him an irreparable injury; it would be like the villany of an assassin, who lurks in darkness to stab his adversary when unarmed and least prepared to meet an enemy.

5. A brother's character I will support in his absence, as I would

in his presence. I will not revile him myself, nor suffer it to be done by others, if it is in my power to prevent it.

Thus, by the five points of fellowship, we are linked together in one indivisible chain of sincere affection, brotherly love, relief, and truth.

GUTTERAL.—The gutteral sign alludes to temperance, which demands such a cautious habit of restraint, as may be necessary to preserve us from the risk of violating our obligation and *incurring its penalty.—Hemming*.

[This alludes to the "Duegard of an Entered Apprentice."]

LANDMARKS.—What are the landmarks? is a question often asked, but never determinately answered. In ancient times, boundary-stones were used as landmarks, before title-deeds were known, the removal of which was strictly forbidden by law. With respect to the landmarks of Masonry, some restrict them to the O. B. signs, tokens, and words. Others include the ceremonies of initiation, passing, and raising; and the form, dimensions, and support; the ground, situation, and covering; the ornaments, furniture, and jewels of a Lodge, or their characteristic symbols. Some think that the Order has no landmarks beyond its peculiar secrets. It is quite clear, however, that the order against removing or altering the landmarks was universally observed in all ages of the Craft.

METAL.—Many men dote on the metals silver and gold with their whole souls, and know no other standard whereby to estimate their own worth, or the worth of their fellow-beings, but by the quantity of these metals they possess, thereby debasing and degrading those qualities of the mind or spirit by which alone mankind ought to be estimated. He who wishes to be initiated into Free Masonry must be willing to relinquish all descriptions of metal, and all the adventitious circumstances of rank and fortune, for it is the MAN that is received into Free Masonry, and not his rank or riches.—*Gadicke*.

ORIGINAL POINTS.—Ancient Masonry admitted twelve original points, which constitute the basis of the entire system, and without which no person ever did or can be legally received into the Order. Every candidate is obliged to pass through all these essential forms and ceremonies, otherwise his initiation would not be legal. They are—opening, preparing, reporting, entering, prayer, circumambulation, advancing, obligation, intrusted, invested, placed, closing.

PENAL.—The penal sign marks our obligation, and reminds us also of the fall of Adam, and the dreadful penalty entailed thereby on his sinful posterity, being no less than death. It intimates that the stiff neck of the disobedient shall be cut off from the land of the living by the judgment of God, even as the head is severed from the body by the sword of human justice.

[This applies as well to the Entered Apprentice's as to the Royal Arch Mason's "Duegard."]

PHRASES OF ADMISSION.—When a candidate receives the first Degree he is said to be *initiated*, at the second step he is *passed*, at the third, *raised*; when he takes the Mark Degree, he is *congratulated* (advanced); having passed the chair, he is said to have *presided*; when he becomes a Most Excellent Master, he is *acknowledged* and *received*; and when a Royal Arch Mason, he is *exalted*.

SIGN OF DISTRESS.—In a society whose members ought fraternally to love and assist each other, it is to be expected that they should have a sign whereby they could make themselves known immediately to their brethren, in however distressed circumstances they might be placed, and thereby at the same time claim their assistance and protection. This is the sign of distress, in conjunction with a few words. He who falls into the greatest difficulty and danger, and supposes that there is a brother within sight or hearing, let him use this sign, and a true and faithful brother must spring to his assistance.—*Gadicke.*

UNIFORMITY.—It is almost unnecessary to argue the question in relation to Uniformity of Work, because such can never be; we say never, as long as we live up to the teachings of the Fathers and communicate, *orally*, the mysteries to candidates. To obtain uniformity, the work must be written, and that will never be done, so long as Freemasons regard their obligations. A Gen. G. Lodge should be, if the fraternity, at any time foolish enough to sanction such an organization, which they never will, might, in imitation of such bodies among modern associations, attempt for the sake of having uniformity, by its dicta authorize the work to be written, but under no other circumstances could or would such a thing be attempted; and even in that case there would be a general uprising of the craft to prevent such a violation of obligation. Uniformity in all things is not absolutely necessary, nor was it ever so considered. It cannot be expected that different persons will communicate the same ideas in precisely the same language; besides language changes in its import and ideas change with the progress of science and advance of philosophy. It was well enough for the ancients to advance that the sun rises in the East, that this earth is stationary as a tree or a house is stationary, and that the sun moves around this little globe of ours; but the day of these ideas is past. Now, by a change of verbiage, the ideas are expressed consistent with sound philosophical principles, as the sun in the east opens and adorns the day, etc., and thus it must necessarily be in relation to Masonic language and Masonic ideas. The language used to express an idea several thousand years ago, or even a few hundred years ago, would be unintelligible, and not understood. To expect uniformity of language for all time, is a vain expectation, and can never be attained.—*Key Stone.*[1]

VAULT.—Vaults are found in every country of the world as well as in Judea, and were used for secret purposes. Thus Stephens, speaking of some ruins in Yucatan, says: "The only way of descending was to tie a rope around the body, and be lowered by the Indians. In this way I was let down, and almost before my head had passed through the hole, my feet touched the top of a heap of rubbish, high directly under the hole, and falling off at the sides. Clambering down it, I found myself in a round chamber, so filled with rubbish that I could not stand upright. With a candle in my hand, I crawled all round on my hands and knees. The chamber was in the shape of a dome, and had been coated with plaster, most of which had fallen, and now encumbered the ground. The depth could not be ascertained without clearing out the interior."

WAGES.—The tradition respecting the payment of the workmen's wages at the building of Solomon's Temple, may or may not be accurate, as I am ignorant of the authority on which the calculations are founded. Indeed the probability is, that the tradition has been fabricated in a subsequent age, without the existence of any documents to attest its authenticity.

---

[1] This is not taken from Dr. Oliver's Dictionary, but is quoted from a popular Masonic journal, and embodies the sentiments of a great majority of the fraternity.

THE TRIPLE TAU

APPENDIX

NOTE A, page 12.—In some Lodges the Tyler *takes* the sword from the altar.

NOTE B, page 18.—Some Masters repeat the words, "O Lord my God," three times.

NOTE C, page 19.—Masters differ about the proper manner of placing the three lights around the altar. In most Lodges they are placed as represented in the engraving, page 19; but many Masters have them placed thus:

The square represents the altar; the figures 1, 2, and 3, the lights; the letter A, the kneeling candidate, and the letter B, the Master.

NOTE D, page 21.—Some Masters say: "I now declare this Lodge opened in the Third Degree of Masonry *for the dispatch of business.*

NOTE E, page 39.—In spelling this word, "Boaz," always begin with the letter "A," and follow the alphabet down as the letters occur in the word.

NOTE F, page 42.—In some Lodges the reply is: "Try me, and disapprove of me if you can;" in others, "I am willing to be tried."

NOTE G, page 43.—Some say, "In an anteroom adjacent to a Lodge of Entered Apprentice Masons."

NOTE H, page 44.—Some say, "Three times around the Lodge."

NOTE I, page 51.—Some say, "On the highest hills and lowest valleys."

NOTE J, page 89.—In some Lodges, the Deacon omits the single rap (●), and opens the door when the three raps (● ● ●) are given.

NOTE K, page 205.—In most Lodges the candidate does not halt at the Junior Warden's station, but passes on to the Senior Warden.

NOTE L, page 125.—Master says: "I shall now proceed to give and explain to you the several signs and tokens belonging to the Degree." Here the Master places his hands as the candidate's were when he took the oath of a Master (see Fig. 5, page 17), and explains. Makes sign of a Master Mason, and explains. (See Fig. 6, page 18.) Makes the grand hailing sign, and explains. (See Fig. 7, page 18.) Gives grip of a Master Mason, and explains. (See Fig. 16, page 97.) Gives strong grip, and explains. (See Fig. 17, page 120.)

NOTE M, page 235.—The Principal Sojourner should say: "We are of your own brethren and kin—children of the captivity—descendants of those noble Giblemites, we were received and acknowledged Most Excellent Masters at the completion and dedication of the first temple—were present at the destruction of that temple by Nebuchadnezzar, by whom we were carried captives to Babylon, where we remained servants to him and his successors until the reign of Cyrus, King of Persia, by whose order we have been liberated, and have now come up to help, aid, and assist in rebuilding the house of the Lord, without the hope of fee or reward." (See lecture.)

NOTE N, page 236.—Instead of saying: "You surely could not have come thus far unless you were three Most Excellent Masters," etc., the Master of the First Veil should say: "Good men and true you must have been, to have come thus far to promote so noble and good an undertaking, but further you cannot go without my word, sign, and word of explanation." (See lecture.)

NOTE O, page 235.—In some Chapters they only stamp seven times.

NOTE P, page 140.—In some parts of the country the second section of the lecture is continued as follows:

Q. What followed?

A. They travelled as before; and as those, who had pursued a due westerly course from the temple, were returning, one (1) of them, being more weary than the rest, sat down on the brow of a hill to rest and refresh himself, and on rising up caught hold of a sprig of acacia, which easily giving way excited his curiosity; and while they were meditating over this singular circumstance they heard three frightful exclamations from the cleft of an adjacent rock. The first was the voice of Jubelo, exclaiming, "Oh! that my throat had been cut from ear to ear, my tongue torn out by its roots and buried in the sands of the sea at low water mark, where the tide ebbs and flows twice in twenty-four hours, ere I had been accessory to the death of so great and good a man as our Grand Master Hiram Abiff." The second was the voice of Jubela, exclaiming: "Oh! that my left breast had been torn open, my heart plucked from thence and given to the beasts of the field and the birds of the air as a prey, ere I had been accessory to the death of so great and good a man as our Grand Master Hiram Abiff." The third was the voice of Jubelum, exclaiming more horridly than the rest, "It was I that gave him the fatal blow! it was I that slew him! oh! that my body had been severed in twain, my bowels taken from thence and burnt to ashes, the ashes scattered before the four (4) winds of heavens, that no more resemblance might be had, among men or masons, of so vile a wretch as I am, ere I had been accessory to the death of so great and good a man as our Grand Master Hiram Abiff." Upon which, they rushed in, seized, bound, and brought them before King Solomon, who ordered them to be taken without the gates of the city and executed according to their imprecations. They were accordingly put to death.

Q. What followed?

A. King Solomon ordered the twelve fellow crafts to go in search of the body, and if found, to observe whether the master's word, or a key to it, was on or about it.

Q. Where was the body of our Grand Master Hiram Abiff found?

A. A due westerly course from the temple, on the brow of the hill, where our weary brother sat down to rest and refresh himself.

Q. Was the master's word, or a key to it, on or about it?

A. It was not.

Q. What followed?

A. King Solomon then ordered them to go with him to endeavor to raise the body, and ordered that as the master's word was then lost, that the first sign given at the grave, and the first word spoken after the body should be raised, should be adopted for the regulation of all Master Masons' Lodges until future ages should find out the right.

Q. What followed?

A. They returned to the grave, when King Solomon ordered them to take the body by the entered-apprentice grip and see if it could be raised; but on taking the body so it was putrid, it having been dead fifteen days, the skin slipped from the flesh, and it could not be raised.

Q. What followed?

A. King Solomon then ordered them to take it by the fellow-craft grip and see if it could be so raised; but on taking the body by that grip the flesh cleft from the bone, and it could not be so raised.

Q. What followed?

A. King Solomon then took it by the strong grip of a Master Mason, or lion's paw, and raised it on the five (5) points of fellowship, which are foot to foot, knee to knee, breast to breast, hand to back, cheek to cheek, or mouth to ear. Foot to foot, that we will never hesitate to go on foot, and out of our way, to assist a suffering and needy brother; knee to knee, that we will ever remember a brother's welfare in all our adorations to Deity; breast to breast, that we will ever keep in our own breasts a brother's secrets, when communicated to us as such, murder and treason excepted; hand to back, that we will ever be ready to stretch forth our hand to aid and support a fallen brother; cheek to cheek, or mouth to ear, that we will ever whisper good counsel in the ear of a brother, and in the most tender manner remind him of his faults, and endeavor to aid his reformation, and will give him due and timely notice that he may ward off all approaching danger.

Q. What did they do with the body?

A. They carried it to the temple and buried it in due form. And masonic tradition informs us that there was a marble column erected to his memory, upon which was delineated a beautiful virgin weeping; before her lay a book open, in her right hand a sprig of acacia, in her left an urn, and behind her stood Time with his fingers unfolding the ringlets of her hair.

Q. What do these hieroglyphical figures denote?

A. The broken column denotes the untimely death of our Grand Master Hiram Abiff; the beautiful virgin weeping, the temple unfinished; the book open before her, that his virtues lie on perpetual record; the sprig of acacia in her right hand, the timely discovery of his body; the urn in her left, that his ashes were then safely deposited to perpetuate the remembrance of so distinguished a character; Time unfolding the ringlets of her hair, that time, patience, and perseverance accomplish all things.

Q. Have you a sign belonging to this Degree?

A. I have several.

Q. Give me a sign? (Penalty.)

Q. What is that called?

A. The duegard of a Master Mason.

Q. Has that an allusion?

A. It has, to the penalty of my obligation, and when our ancient brethren returned to the grave of our Grand Master Hiram Abiff, they found their hands placed in this position to guard their nostrils from the disagreeable effluvia that arose there from the grave.

Q. Give me a token. (Pass grip.)

Q. What is that called?

A. The pass grip from a fellow craft to a Master Mason.

Q. What is its name?

A. Tubal Cain.

Q. Who was Tubal Cain?

A. The first known artificer or cunning worker in metals.

Q. Pass that?   (Strong grip.)

Q. What is that?

A. The strong grip of a Master Mason, or lion's paw.

Q. Has it a name?

A. It has.

Q. Give it me?

A. I cannot, nor can it be given except on the five (5) points of fellowship, and heard then in a low breath.

Q. Advance and give it.

A. The word is right.

Q. How many grand masonic pillars are there?

A. Three.

Q. What are they called?

A. Wisdom, Strength and Beauty.

Q. Why are they so called?

A. Because it is necessary there should be wisdom to contrive, strength to support, and beauty to adorn, all great and important undertakings.

Q. By whom are they represented?

A. By Solomon, King of Israel, Hiram, King of Tyre, and Hiram Abiff, who were our first three Most Excellent Grand Masters.

Q. Why are they said to represent them?

A. Solomon, King of Israel, represents the pillars of wisdom, because by his wisdom he contrived the superb model of excellence that immortalized his name; Hiram, King of Tyre, represents the pillar of strength, because he supported King Solomon in this great and important undertaking; Hiram Abiff represents the pillar of beauty, because by his cunning workmanship, the temple was beautified and adorned.

Q. What supported the temple?

A. It was supported by 1453 columns and 2906 pilasters, all hewn from the finest Parian marble.

Q. How many were employed in building the temple?

A. Three Grand Masters, three thousand three hundred masters, or overseers of the work, eighty thousand fellow crafts in the mountains and in the quarries, and seventy (70) thousand entered apprentices, or bearers of burdens. All these were classed and arranged in such a manner by the wisdom of King Solomon, that neither envy, discord, nor confusion was suffered to interrupt that universal peace and tranquillity which pervaded the world at this important period.

Q. What is meant by the three steps usually delineated on the Master's carpet?

A. They are emblematical of the three principal stages of human life, viz.: youth, manhood, and age, etc., etc. (Monitorial.)

Q. How many classes of Master's emblems are there?

A. Nine.

Q. What is the ninth (9th)?

A. The setting maul, spade, coffin, and sprig of acacia. The setting maul was that by which our Grand Master Hiram Abiff was slain; the spade was that which dug his grave; the coffin was that which received his remains, and the sprig of acacia was that which bloomed at the head of his grave. These are all striking emblems of morality, and afford serious reflections to a thinking mind; but they would be still more repining were it not for the sprig of acacia that bloomed at the head of the grave, which serves to remind us of that imperishable part of man which survives the grave and bears the nearest affinity to the Supreme Intelligence which pervades all nature, and which can never, never, never die. Then, finally, my brethren, let us imitate our Grand Master Hiram Abiff in his virtuous conduct, his unfeigned piety to his God, and his inflexible fidelity to his trust, that like him we may welcome the grim tyrant Death, and receive him as a kind messenger, sent by our Supreme Grand Master to translate us from this imperfect to that all perfect, glorious, and celestial lodge above, where the Supreme Architect of the universe presides.

NOTE Q., page 148. — (*Extract from the Annual Address of M. W. P. M. Tucker, G. M. of Vermont.*)

In my address of last year I endeavored to condense what little information I had about the Masonic lectures, and that attempt has been, in general, quite favorably noticed by the Craft. In one distinguished Masonic quarter, however, some parts of my address on this subject seem to have met with marked disfavor. One particular thing found fault with is, that I thought myself justified in saying that the lectures in use, received through Webb and Gleason, were the *true* lectures of Preston. I certainly did not mean to say that they were identical in *length* with those of Preston. I had already said that Webb changed the arrangement of Preston's sections, but that he had left the body of the lectures as Preston had established them. Perhaps I should have said, the *substance* instead of the *"body"* of those lectures. I now state, what I supposed was well understood before by every tolerably well-informed Mason in the United States, that Webb *abridged* as well as *changed the ar-*

rangement of the lectures of Preston. I believed that I knew *then,* and I believe I know *now,* that Webb learned and taught the Preston lectures *in full,* as well as that he prepared and taught his own abridgment of them. I have a copy in key, both of Webb's abridgment and of Preston in full, which I have reasons, wholly satisfactory to myself, for believing are true manuscripts of both those sets of lectures, as Gleason taught them. But my reviewer has got the "very rare" book of a certain J. Browne, published in London in 1802, called the "Master Key," containing the *whole* course of lectures in an "abstruse cypher," and *presumes* them to be the Prestonian lectures. Reviewers, it seems, tolerate "presumption" in themselves, while nothing short of demonstration is allowable with them as to others, who are required to speak from "their own knowledge." I am ready to compare my copy of the Preston lectures in *full* with J Browne's "*Master Key,*" if my reviewer understands Browne's "abstruse cypher,"—a fact about which he has not yet informed us. Again, I am criticized for saying that Gleason visited England and exemplified the Preston lectures, as he had received them from Webb, before the Grand Lodge of England, whose authorities pronounced them correct, and I am charged with taking this from "hearsay," and my critic places "no faith in it." I received that statement from the *highest* authority—from one who *knew*—and I wrote it down at the time. There are existing reasons why I do not choose to gratify my critic by naming that authority at this time, and I leave the Craft to judge whether my *statement* of that fact, upon undoubted authority, is not worthy of as much credit as *any* reviewer's *doubt* about it. I do not possess anything in writing or published of Gleason's, as to his lecturing before the *Grand Lodge* of England, but that Masonry abroad did not ignore the lectures, as Gleason taught them, we have his own published letter to prove. In the 2d edition of the Masonic Trestleboard, under the date of Nov. 26th, 1843, in a letter from him to Brother Charles W. Moore, I find the following language:

"It was my privilege, while at Brown University, Providence, R. I., (1801/2), to acquire a complete knowledge of the lectures,in the *three* first degrees of Masoury, *directly* from our much esteemed Brother T. S. Webb, author of tho Free Mason's Monitor; and, in consequence, was appointed and commissioned by the Grand Lodge of Massachusetts and Maine, Grand Lecturer, devoting the whole time to the instruction of tho Lodges under the jurisdiction,—and, for many years subsequently (as Professor of Astronomy and Geography), visiting all the different States in the Union, and (1829/30) many parts of Europe—successfully communicating, to numerous Lodges and Associations of Brethren, the same 'valuable lectures of the Craft,' according to the ancient landmarks."

Here, then, we have the assertion of Gleason himself, that the lectures he received from Webb were, "in many parts of Europe," as well as in the States at home, communicated by him to "numerous Lodges and Associations of Brethren, according to the ancient landmarks," without the slightest hint or intimation of any objection being made to them abroad, as not being the true lectures of the Order. This is, at least, *prima facie* evidence of their having been substantially what I claimed them to be. But if I am still told that it carries no conclusive evidence that Brother Gleason knew anything of the *true* Preston lectures, I call that brother upon the stand again. On the 24th day of June, 1812, "Brother Benjamin Gleason, A. M.," delivered an "*Oration*" at "Montreal, Lower Canada," before St. Paul's Lodge No. 12, and Union Lodge No. 8, by "special request" of the former Lodge. It was published at Montreal, and a second edition of it was soon after published at Boston. I copy from this second edition the following remarks of Brother Gleason:

"On the subject of our Lectures, we notice with pleasure, this day, the venerable Preston of England, whose 'Illustrations of Masonry' redound to the honor of the Craft, and whose *estimable system of improvements*, while with precision and certainty they define, with purity and eloquence, aggrandize, the immovable *landmarks* of our ancient Society."

Brother Gleason then, *did*, upon his own statement, understand Preston's "estimable system of improvements," their "precision and certainty," their "purity and elegance," and their relation to our "immovable landmarks." And with these and Webb's teachings fully in his mind, was probably as good a judge as any modern critic, of the relations they bore to each other. Can any reasonable man, in this state of things, believe that if they had *conflicted* with each other he did not know it, or that, if conflicting, he would have taught *both;* or that he could have taught either "in Europe" without objection, had they not been substantially the *same* teachings, differing only in their *length?*

But my critic says:—"It is wrong to talk in this careless strain of the Prestonian lectures as existing in the United States, while in all probability they never did, and most certainly never will. It is time to quit writing Masonic history in this loose and random style."

It is no part of my purpose to *convince* my reviewer that the "Prestonian lectures" exist in the United States, or to *persuade* him, that (though confessedly a strong Masonic writer), he does not quite embody in his learning *all* the Masonry of this Western continent. His liberality might perhaps concede that, *among* all who have made Masonry a study, or with their *united* investigations, enough of Masonic learning *might* have been preserved to make itself respected at least as against simple negation. But I do not write to *convince* or satisfy *him*. I do so that the Craft may have an opportunity to understand something of their own affairs, as they exist; to examine and investigate them as matters of fact and principle; and that they may have no apology for "pinning their faith" upon the mere negations of any writer, whatever may be the strength of his masonic reputation. In an account of the Installation of Mount Lebanon Lodge at Boston, on the 29th of December, 1858, Brother Charles W. Moore, Editor of the *Freemasons' Monthly Magazine*, has the following remarks: "Among the Past Masters of this Lodge we notice the name of the late Benjamin Gleason, Esq., who was the associate and co-laborer of the late Thomas Smith Webb, in introducing into the Lodges of New England, and subsequently into other sections of the country, what is known as the Prestonian system of work and lectures. The labor of promulgating the work mainly devolved on Brother Gleason, and it is not too much to say, that as an accurate, consistent, and intelligent teacher, he had no superior, if an equal, in this country. He was a thoroughly educated man, and he understood the literary as well as the mental requirements necessary to a faithful and creditable discharge of the important duty he had assumed. In 1804, the Grand Lodge of Massachusetts adopted the Preston ritual as its standard of work, and employed Brother Gleason to communicate it to the Lodges under its jurisdiction, then including what is now the State of Maine. In the performance of this duty, he was exclusively employed during the whole of the year named, on account of the Grand Lodge; and we think a large part of the following two or three years, on his own private account. Indeed he never ceased his labors, as a lecturer, until his death in 1847, and there are many brethren now living—among them myself—who will ever take pride in remembering and acknowledging him as their master and teacher, in the purest and most perfect Masonic ritual of ancient Craft Masonry ever practised in this country. It was the work' of Masonry, as revived by Preston, and approved and sanctioned by the Grand Lodge of England, near the close of the last century, and practised by authority of that body, until the 'union' in 1813, when, for the purpose of reconciliation, it was subjugated to a revision, which, in some respects, proved to be an unfortunate one, inasmuch as the revised system, though exceedingly beautiful, has so many incongruities and departures from the original, and is so elaborate withal, that it has never met with that cordial approval, even among our English brethren, which is necessary to its recognition and acceptance as a universal system. The verbal ritual, as revised by Preston, was brought to this country about the year 1803—not by Webb, as we have seen it stated, for he never went abroad—but by two English brethren, one of whom, we think, had been a pupil of Preston, and both of whom had been members of one of the principal Lodges of Instruction in London. It was first communicated to Webb, and by him imparted to Gleason, who was at the time a student in Brown University, at Providence, and being an intelligent and zealous brother, became a favorite of Webb, who was his senior both in years and in Masonry. On being submitted to the Grand Lodge of this Commonwealth it was approved and adopted, and Brother Gleason was employed to impart it to the Lodges, as before stated. From that time to the present it has been the only recognized Masonic work of Massachusetts, and though we are not unmindful that many unwarrantable liberties have been taken with it, and that innovations have crept in, which would have been better out—yet, as a whole, we are happy to know that it has been preserved in the Lodges of this city—and in view of the recent instructions, by authority of the Grand Lodge, we may add, the Lodges of this Commonwealth —in a remarkable degree of purity; and that it is still taught in the Lodge of which, in 1809, Brother Gleason was Master, with so close a resemblance to the original, that if it were possible for him to be present at the conferring of the degrees to-day, he would find very little to object to in the work of his successors. The system underwent some modifications (which were doubtless improvements) in its general arrangement and adaptation—its mechanism—soon after its introduction into this country; but in all other respects it was received, and has been preserved, especially in the Lodges of the older jurisdictions, essentially, as it came from the original source of all our Craft Masonry. In many parts of the country it has hitherto had to contend against the corrupting influences of ignorant itinerant lecturers and spurious publications; but it is believed that an effectual check has been put to this class of dangerous evils, and that they will hereafter be treated as they deserve. If so, we may reasonably hope to be able to preserve the ritual, and transmit it to our successors, in something like its original purity, but not otherwise." We have, then, added to Gleason's own assertion as to his knowledge of Preston's "estimable system of improvements," the statement of one of the most intelligent and reliable Masons in this country, that Webb had "the Prestonian system of work and lectures," and that the labor of promulgating them "mainly devolved on Brother Gleason." And I wholly content to let that evidence stand as my authority and justification against the remarks of a reviewer who accuses me of "talking in a careless strain" when I maintain that these lectures exist in the United States.

Our Grand Lecturer has compared, with critical care, my copy of the Preston with that of the Gleason Lectures. I have not had sufficient leisure since the former has been in my possession, to compare them, as fully as I design to do hereafter. The Preston Lectures are very lengthy, and if written out in full the Grand Lecturer thinks they would cover nearly one hundred pages of foolscap paper. He thinks them wholly too long for ordinary use, and that if all Masons were required to commit them *in extenso*, it would be a task which very few would successfully accomplish; and so far as my own examination has gone, I entertain the same opinion. The Grand Lecturer also entertains the opinion that Webb has preserved, in the abridgment and new arrangement of them, all that was substantially of practical value, and that the language used by him is preferable to much that was used by Preston.

I regret to say that in the criticism of which I have spoken, there appears a most palpable intention to undervalue *all* the lectures of Masonry. The believers in the importance of preserving the lectures intact are sneered at; called "parrot Masons," who, taken off the "beaten path," know "nothing at all of Masonry, of its history, its philosophy, or its symbolism." And we are dismissed with the cool remark—"Let us talk more, therefore, of the philosophy of Masonry, and something less of the Lectures of Webb," and as opposed to the idea of the importance of the Lectures, we are called on, "in Heaven's name, to inaugurate a new era."

This is, at least, sufficiently cool for a teacher of Freemasonry. "Inaugurate a *new* era." That is the idea precisely. Some of us ignorant Masons had supposed that, at least, some portion of our Masonic "history, philosophy, and symbolism," was *suggested* in our Lectures. Our "history"—written and unwritten—the "philosophy" of our system, and something of our "symbolism," were imagined to be secure in the past. But a "new era." About what? Can our "*history*" be changed; can our "*philosophy*" be changed? Not a million of critics, however distinguished, can brush the first particle of consecrated dust from either. "There they stand, and there they will stand forever—unshaken by the tests of human scrutiny, of talents and of time."

THE END

OTHER MASONIC TITLES

A Dictionary of Freemasonry
Freemasonry and its Etiquette
Freemasonry at a Glance (Answers to 555 Questions)
Freemasonry Character Claims
Morals and Dogma of Freemasonry
Order of the Eastern Star
Revised Duncan's Ritual Vol. 1
Revised Duncan's Ritual Vol. 2
Revised Knight Templarism Illustrated
Scottish Rites Masonry Vol. 1
Scottish Rites Masonry Vol. 2
Secret Societies Illustrated
The History of Freemasonry
The Illustrated History of Freemasonry

MASONIC RELATED TITLES:

Freemasonry and Judaism
Freemasonry Interpreted
Freemasonry and the Vatican

WWW.LUSHENABKS.COM

NOTES

NOTES

NOTES

NOTES

NOTES

NOTES

220811-200-1-60W